Teachers and Therapy Dog Teams:

Innovative Collaborations to Make a Difference for Children

Barbara Vokatis and Lucinda Ormiston

Copyright © 2023 SchoolRubric Inc.

All rights reserved.

ISBN: 978-1-7378643-7-0

DEDICATION

We dedicate this book to all teachers and therapy dog teams whose love for children inspires them to work together for children's countless benefits.

ACKNOWLEDGMENTS

We would like to thank our wonderful families, therapy dog owners - Marcia, Erica, and Emily - for the time they devoted to being interviewed for this book, Abedulrahman Abou Dahesh for his help on the oxytocin section, Richard Siegel and Katie Baron for their help in editing, and Wallace Ting from SchoolRubric for his enthusiasm to publish this book.

PRAISE FOR THIS BOOK

"Teachers and Therapy Dog Teams" is an insightful and comprehensive guide that explores the integration of therapy dogs in educational settings. Dr. Vokatis and Mrs. Ormiston skillfully examine the positive impact that therapy dogs have on students' emotional well-being, academic performance, and overall classroom dynamics. By drawing on research studies, and personal anecdotes the book offers a compelling case for the inclusion of therapy dogs as valuable educational resources. One of the book's strengths is its emphasis on the diverse ways therapy dogs can enhance the learning environment. The authors' passion for the topic shines through, as they skillfully balance scientific research with practical anecdotes and insights.

- Cara Zelas, Educator & Founder of Big World of Little Dude

Dr. Barb Vokatis is a passionate educator who found a way to innovate in the classroom with her Therapy Dog Carmel. She generously shares her story and lesson plans for Animal Assisted Education in this collaboration with Lucinda, a teacher she's partnered with closely in this work. One of the needs I hear over and over again when talking with professionals partnering in Animal Assisted Therapy is ideas for interventions. This book meets those needs for those in educational environments and I look forward to seeing how this evolves as more instructors implement these into their work and continue to build on top of these ideas.

- Sherrie Rohde, Certified Animal-Assisted Intervention Specialist and Host of Therapy Dog Talk

Barb describes how Carmel becomes the conduit for learning. Students feel more relaxed and at ease completing math problems, and their learning relates to real-world application as they use kibble to practice addition facts. She also provides easy-to-follow step-by-step directions to incorporate literacy and writing skills as students incorporate dog themes to write personal biographies. The interactions they have with Carmel teach them about kindness toward others. Ultimately, the therapy dog encourages learners and helps them to become more successful, academically and socially. I encourage you to read this book, to consider becoming part of the therapy dog world, or at least, to invite therapy dog partners into your classroom or facility. Dogs can teach the art of socialization and can be catalyst for expression, and confidence.

– Dr. Ann Frankin-Hayslip (SUNY Oneonta)

TEACHERS AND DOG THERAPY TEAMS

The collaborative work of Barb and Carmel with educators shows us the power of authentic learning. Carmel stepping in a learning space helps to refresh our curiosity, thinking, and imagination for children and adults alike. The stories demonstrate how we may reconnect with one another and with the world with a caring heart and an inquisitive mind.

- Dr. Jianwei Zhang (Associate Professor of Learning Sciences and Technology, University at Albany)

Rarely does a book bridge the research practice gap like Dr. Barb Vokatis and Carmel's efforts! With the crisis of mental health among students and professionals, this timely work is necessary and critical. Reading the work, professionals see informative, easy-to-implement, and necessary efforts. Dr. Vokatis and Carmel created joy in the classroom. What is most impressive about Teachers and Therapy Dog Teams are the literacy activities described and integrated into the experiences of this amazing team. The section on math and therapy dogs was easy to comprehend, has foundational skill activities, and is creative for very busy teachers. Dr. Vokatis created a resource-rich, socio-emotional learning resource for every teacher and school.

- Dr. Casey Jakubowski (University of Maryland Eastern Shore)

Via Instagram, Barbara has shared many inspiring ways to leverage therapy dogs in the classroom that I have used with my 5th graders. This book, however, goes far beyond helpful tips and inspiring stories. I love what Barbara, Carmel, and Lucinda have been able to do. The engagement with reading and writing that was fostered in those children will last a lifetime. Barbara, Carmel, and Lucinda have discovered a great treasure of therapy dog facilitated learning and identified the key to unlocking that treasure – consistent, supportive relationships between the children, the therapy dog team and the teacher. Barbara has simplified the process by including detailed lesson plans. This book has opened my eyes to how much more a therapy dog team can do to improve learning in the classroom when the teacher and therapy dog team work together.

– Katie Baron and Archer, Therapy Dog Team

This book about therapy dogs in classrooms as a means to create an environment where students are engaged in meaningful literacy tasks is a transformative pedagogy. Reading the book made me think deeply about how my own demeanor shifts from anxiety to one of calmness when my dogs are around and how that change in mindset is what I need when working on cognitive tasks that often seem overwhelming. Learners, whether children or adults, need to be in the right mental space in order to be productive. Dogs in the classroom are a sure way of creating an optimal mental state for creative academic work.

- Dr. Paul Bischoff, Professor of Secondary Education, SUNY-Oneonta

Table of Contents

Introduction	1
Why this book	4
Some possible fears in adopting dog therapy and their solutions	10
Two crucial aspects of the innovative dog therapy	13
Literacy/Dog Therapy Lab in diverse classrooms and across content areas	16
Barbara Vokatis' journey to dog therapy	18
Lucinda Ormiston's journey to classroom with dog therapy	21
The pathway to the Literacy/Dog Therapy Lab	28
Overview of the activities	34
Writing activities	36
Kindness	36
Visualization	38
Biography/Autobiography/Memoir	41
Book cover	43
Dedication and introduction	45
First chapter	48
Author's bio for back cover	50
Math activities	52
Place value	52
Addition 1-12	54
Addition 1-20	56
Addition game with the therapy dog	58
Subtraction 1-20	61

Estimation and map skills	63
Beginning fractions	65
Final thoughts	67
How to easily self-publish a book	68
Some books with the therapy dogs theme	69
Permission slip to participate in therapy dog visits (example)	71
References	75
Interview with therapy dog teams	80

INTRODUCTION

Dear Reader,

If you are a teacher, a parent, teacher educator, school principal, or have a therapy dog visiting educational settings, this book is for you. We wrote it to offer simple, yet creative, ways of incorporating dog therapy in classrooms. These therapy visits will offer students ways to comfort and destress, in addition to having the students pet and read to dogs. Activities described in this book, if implemented with enthusiasm and collaboration by both teachers and therapy teams, have a high potential to turn reluctant writers into engaged writers who see writing as a powerful tool in their lives. In addition, we include activities that can help children who struggle with math find math more meaningful and engaging.

We know that this promise sounds too good to be true, but we have truly experienced this phenomenon ourselves as a collaborating team of a teacher and a therapy dog owner. All it takes is the teacher, the therapy dog team, and the learners to create meaningful relationships. This relationship becomes a crucial seed that can grow into a full scale of social, emotional, and academic achievements within the dog therapy classroom community. This is especially the case when the collaborating teacher and dog therapy team nurture creative teaching ideas together. Lucinda, the teacher who welcomed me into her classroom, had this to say about a student who was struggling to follow rules: "Carmel really calmed him... instead of jumping all over the room and yelling out, he actually had his hand raised and he waited. Oh my goodness, it was like he knew that if he acted out, then it would upset Carmel. He didn't do that so it was awesome."

In addition, Lucinda noticed that children in her classroom became more respectful and engaged collaborators who wanted to work with other children. She mentioned this about two children: "They don't normally play together, and they said 'Look, we're writing a book together.'" It was also apparent that children learned about the importance of respecting each other because they saw how Carmel respected others and wanted to apply Carmel's behavior to themselves. Lucinda noted about this: "They'll refer to her [Carmel] in class…they'll be like, 'You know how Carmel's nice to us? We need to be nice to each other.' They've actually been nice to each other since we talked about that… they've referred to that moment."

When it comes to children's writing engagement, both Lucinda and I observed its amazing growth. For instance, children who would not even write a sentence asked if they could write books. Lucinda recalls when one of her students approached her, "Miss Ormiston, will you help me make a book? [...]' 'Yeah, I want to write a book about me."

Of course, it is important that the teacher also cultivates an open-to-experimentation and innovation mindset and can let go of some control. However, once the immediate impact of the therapy dog inclusion becomes visible, letting some of that control go will be considered beneficial. It is not required for the therapy dog owner to have a background in education, as many activities are relatively simple to implement with the teacher collaborator's input and help. Therefore, if you seek ways of engaging young writers, readers, and mathematicians, please do not hesitate to read this book in order to implement these ideas on your own, or to share them with other teachers and dog therapy teams.

This book is also for those who are reluctant to invite therapy dog teams to schools because they fear that many children are allergic to dogs. However, it is possible to organize dog therapy visits in such ways that they become safe for everyone.

The book consists of three parts. In the first part, we discuss the nature of my collaboration with Lucinda and her classrooms. In the second part, we provide mini lessons that can be used in order to incorporate dog therapy into writing and math activities. For the third part, I interview three dog therapy teams to provide more insight into dog therapy from multiple perspectives, not just mine.

Why This Book

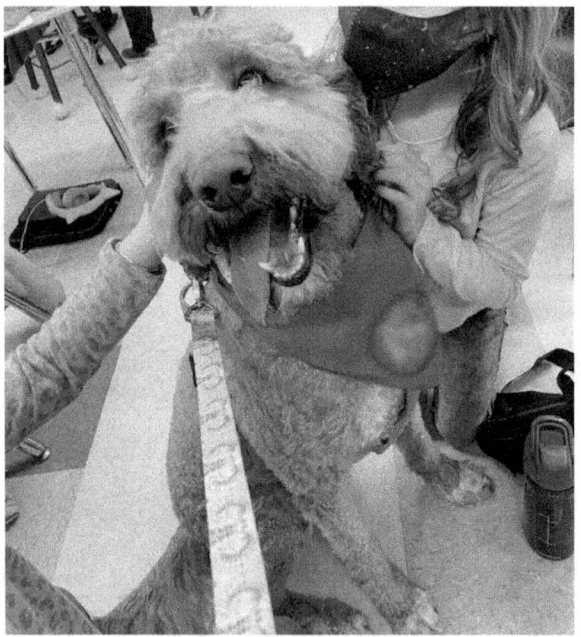

Carmel in Lucinda's classroom in 2021

In order to answer this question, we need to define the term "therapy dog" first. According to the definition by American Kennel Club, "Therapy dogs are dogs who go with their owners to volunteer in settings such as schools, hospitals, and nursing homes" (American Kennel Club, n.d.). The organization further describes: "From working with a child who is learning to read to visiting a senior in assisted living, therapy dogs and their owners work together as a team to improve the lives of other people" (American Kennel Club, n.d.). Please note that a therapy dog is not an emotional support animal and is not a service dog. Emotional support animals are dedicated to one person's mental wellbeing and service dogs perform a specific task related to a person's disability. Therapy dogs support many people in many different situations, which requires a much different skill set.

It also needs to be noted that teachers can bring their own certified therapy dogs into their own classrooms. In such cases, the dog can stay in the classroom all day long a couple of times per week and spend instructional time with children for math, ELA, writing, remedial reading time, and science. During breaks (when children go to art, music, gym, library, or chorus), the teacher can take the dog to visit other classrooms. Students usually read to the dog, work next to the dog, or the dog will circulate the room and visit them while they work. Other teachers can pop in throughout the day, especially teachers who have learners with special needs. A lot of times, the students spend time with the dog quietly while his owner is teaching his/her class. The teachers appreciate such dogs just as much as the children do. A lot of times they will stop by to pet the dog and snuggle with him or her on their breaks or lunch time.

Research has documented positive results of dog therapy in schools, nursing homes, and medical facilities (Braun et al., 2009; Gawlinski & Steers, 2005). The benefits documented in research span across social benefits, cognitive benefits (Jalongo at al., 2004), emotional and mental ones (Baird at al., 2022; Barker & Dawson, 1998; Coakley & Mahoney, 2009); however, not much is known about more creative integration of dog therapy with the learning curriculum, beyond reading to therapy dogs.

Benefits for children in educational settings show that therapy dog teams have a potential to influence children's socio-emotional and cognitive spheres (Beetz, 2015). Therapy dogs' positive influence on children's reading skills are especially well observed and documented (Bassette & Taber-Doughty, 2013; Booten, 2011; Briggs, 2003; Burns & DiLonardo, 2014; Dunlap, 2010; Garnto, 2014; Hall at al., 2016; Le Roux et al., 2014), including a positive impact on reading for children with disabilities (Griess, 2010). I discuss some of those benefits in my previous book, "The amazing power of dog therapy: How my therapy dog transformed children's learning" (Vokatis, 2021).

Programs such as R.E.A.D. are based on the premise that reading to a dog helps to overcome anxiety and increase motivation to read. The silent companionship of a dog as a reading partner may allow the child to work comfortably through reading challenges without fear of being judged. Evidence suggests that improving reading motivation can lead to improving reading itself (Guthrie, 2004; Nevo & Vaknin-Nusbaum, 2020). In one study, researchers observed more confidence in children's reading including confidence in reading words, which is linked to motivation to read (Sorin et al., 2015). This connection may be especially crucial for students who are struggling readers who often lack motivation to read (Wigfield at al. 2016) and exhibit increased reading anxiety (Jalongo at al., 2004). Evidence also suggests that positive experiences can help the child overcome negative associations and be more open to learning experiences (Amsterlaw et al., 2009).

However, there are not many sound, randomized research studies that prove such causation. Although many papers suggest improvements to the children's behavioral processes, which may improve the learning environment, and therefore lead to better learning outcomes, the quality of the evidence is based on ad-hoc reports that have not been through a peer-review process. Conclusions are also based on inferences from small sample sizes and these are not longitudinal studies. As far as the causal link between confidence and interactions with dogs, there is almost no research. Only a single conference paper shows a possible causal effect of the dog over time and shows improvement of self-esteem in children over a nine-month period in comparison to a control group (Bergesen, 1989). Other studies suggest that the presence of a dog may reduce physiological parameters of stress, decreasing blood pressure when reading to a dog (Friedmann et al., 1983) and reducing cortisol awakening in children with insecure attachment (Beetz et al., 2012) and with autism (Viau et al., 2010). These effects were observed in comparison to a control condition.

Even though benefits of dog therapy in educational settings are well known, very little is known how such dog therapy teams might impact students' writing achievement, influence children's thinking about their life goals, and even help them in learning math. According to Lucinda: One student is "taking off with the writing. He did not want to write at the beginning of the year. Oh my God, I could not give him to write, but he loves it. He's so into it. [He often asks] can we work more on this? I sa[y], we have to get through the rest of our stuff, but every day now we are going to have a little time to spend on writing." One of the students said in the interview, "When I get older, I'm going to write a couple thousand books."

Very little is also known about experimenting in the area of dog therapy beyond activities such as children reading to therapy dogs, in order to see to what extent creative and experimental ways of incorporating dog therapy might impact children. This is to include those children who experience difficulties with learning, and especially in the area of writing motivation and learning math, along with children with various disabilities. This book, written after experimenting with dog therapy in Lucinda's classroom in order to make it as meaningful and beneficial for children as possible, offers such new directions and creative activities. Therefore, we believe that the book offers a potential that can truly transform children's learning and even lives, thus substantially helping teachers carry out their teaching. As a result, parents and educators will see happier and more motivated children, as well.

As we also know, during the Covid-19 pandemic, schools were particularly affected by isolation caused by social distancing and learning online. Lucinda even noticed that her students were "pretty far behind in their writing skills... I'm catching them up, but their writing is very far behind."

During that time, therapy dog teams couldn't go in person to offer dog therapy. I still remember the day when both my daughter's school and my college classes went remote and therapy dog visits got canceled without any idea when they could resume. It was very hard to accept that I could not bring my therapy dog, Carmel, to school.

But, I had an idea. I ordered special cardboard cutouts that had the image of Carmel to create a symbolic and visual representation of her presence in school. In this way, children could see the image in the main office and some classrooms. But after a certain period of time and doing dog therapy remotely, when therapy teams were allowed back to schools, it was clear that therapy dog visits have an amazing potential to help everyone heal even deep emotional scars left after the pandemic isolation. Children who learned virtually and whom we visited remotely always could not wait to see Carmel on their screens and learn about her day and activities. When they learned they would be able to meet Carmel personally, they were delighted.

At first, Carmel and I were allowed to visit with children outside, in front of the school at the end of the 2021 school year. Then, when we were allowed to return to the building, I saw these emotions of joy on both children's and teachers' faces when Carmel and I entered. This was the moment I really realized that the value of dog therapy cannot be underestimated. Due to online learning throughout the pandemic, children were lacking in both emotional and literacy skills. Lucinda observed that, particularly in the area of writing, her second graders' skills were quite weak compared to what they should be. That is one of the reasons we both thought that focusing on motivating children to write would be very beneficial.

The field of neurochemistry also contributes to highlighting benefits of dog therapy. Specifically, it provides tangible proof of changes in the brain as a result of interactions with the therapy dog. Such interactions decrease stress and increase calmness because when children pet a therapy dog, their brain releases a hormone called oxytocin. According to oxytocin researcher Professor Kerstin Uvnäs Moberg, this hormone plays two important functions (2011). First, oxytocin influences human behavior to become more social in interactions with others. Second, oxytocin reduces stress levels and eliminates feelings of anxiety, thus changing physiology and creating a sensation of calmness in response to sensory stimulation. This hormone plays a big role during not only positive interaction between mothers and their children or between adults but also between humans and animals (Uvnäs-Moberg et al., 2015). Wilson's (1991) study showed that dogs can arouse a branch of the nervous system, known as sympathetic nervous system, by providing a pleasant external focus of attention, promoting feelings of safety and providing a source of contact comfort, thus raising the levels of oxytocin.

Moreover, as educators in various roles in the educational field, both Lucinda and I have seen many different agendas and heard many voices in many discussions on education. We also asked ourselves which voices truly care about how to improve children's learning and give them potential they certainly deserve. We have noticed countless times that educational programs alone, no matter how expensive, cannot substitute for teachers' expertise (Darling-Hammond, 2000; Goe & Stickler, 2008; Allington, 2013). In addition, when teachers' love for children and their expertise are also infused with some teaching experimentation, children's learning can reach extraordinary levels, thus resulting in outcomes that are desirable for both parents and schools (Vokatis & Zhang, 2016, Zhang at al., 2023).

SOME POSSIBLE FEARS IN ADOPTING DOG THERAPY AND THEIR SOLUTIONS

Carmel in Lucinda's classroom in 2021

Any dog breed and almost at any age can be an excellent therapy dog for children, as Marcia and Emily discuss in an interview at the end of the book. This is more about the temperament dogs display, which are not characteristics of only specific breeds. The most important thing is that the dog has a calm, friendly disposition. As far as the age of dogs, therapy dogs must be at least a year old and owners should look for signs in their older dogs to see if they need to retire them. For instance, when the dog does not seem to enjoy interactions as much any more at the facilities or gets tired during therapy visits, these might be a sign that the dog might need to retire. This is discussed more in the interview at the end of the book.

In addition, we would like to counter some hesitancy coming from some school administrators who might reject the idea of trying this therapy due to a fear of not knowing how to handle such visits if children allergic to dogs are involved. Our advice is for the teacher to communicate with parents about such cases and even go beyond that by sending a survey home to find out about children's experiences with dogs. This gathered information will substantially help in planning and facilitating such activities to ensure safety for every involved child. We include such a sample of a questionnaire at the end of the book.

It is also possible to address a situation in which only one child is allergic to dogs or is afraid of dogs, but no one else is. A conference with the parent would be especially useful here. In such a situation, a further conversation with the parent might help to see if the dog can still be in the same classroom, along with the child with allergies. The child would just not touch and pet the dog. For a child who is afraid of dogs, a conference with the parent will be equally as important. The therapy team might be able to meet individually and gradually introduce the dog to the child. If a child does not want to be around the dog at all, additional activities for these children can be set up with a teacher aid or another qualified adult.

Some readers might also wonder what would happen in the unfortunate event of a therapy dog's death. Therapy dog teams certainly need to be prepared for such an occurrence. This unlikely, but possible event, would need to be discussed with the school in advance to come up with an action plan that both the therapy team and school personnel agree to. Since many schools have counselors, someone would always be available to handle such a situation and provide guidance.

If the dog were to bite a child, such an event would be handled by the school nurse who would follow the protocol of the school district. Therapy dogs are certified and approved by their therapy organizations. Therapy dog teams must undergo required tests and vaccinations every year. Each therapy organization also has rules pertaining to handling such incidents. For instance, the dog would need to be removed from the area and the injured person would be provided with the help they need. In addition, the school and parents would need to be notified. The incident should be also reported to the therapy organization immediately.

These questions, and more, are answered in more depth at an interview at the end of the book. I interviewed three therapy dog teams, and got their viewpoints about these various topics.

TWO CRUCIAL ASPECTS OF THE INNOVATIVE DOG THERAPY

Carmel with the children who wrote autobiographies in Lucinda's class in 2022

Two important factors are important in order to put the approach described in our book into practice: 1. the therapy dog owner's own simple book about how the dog and owner became a team. If the owner did not write a book, they can use one that is already written. The book should be used to actively engage children in reading and writing activities. and 2. a close and meaningful collaboration between a teacher and therapy dog team.

First, if the therapy dog owner chooses to write and self-publish a simple book prior to starting activities with children, such a book can be a memoir that details the journey from puppyhood to becoming a therapy dog, similar to my own book I wrote: "From unruly to therapy dog: The amazing journey" (Vokatis, 2021).

Self-publishing a book will help children see the therapy dog owner as a class friend for whom writing is important in life. This act of publishing will significantly help the therapy dog owner take an active stance as a facilitator of children's learning within the dog therapy classroom community.

When the therapy dog owner takes an active stance as a writer and facilitator of learning activities tied to his or her book, learning and motivation to learn becomes quite different for students because teaching and learning is not tied to the teacher authority alone any more, but to the dog owner who has a different role and identity. For the children in Lucinda's second grade classroom, I was a classroom friend, as I was someone who brought the dog loved by children to the classroom so that they could interact with her.

But not every therapy dog owner will want to write a book and that is perfectly fine. Writing a blog or a story can also provide a similar writing and dog therapy connection. The teacher and therapy dog owner can even co-author a writing piece together. Or the therapy dog team can simply read a book about therapy dogs written by someone else. At the end of the book, in the *Some Books with the Therapy Dogs Theme* section, we provide a list of books about therapy dogs that can be utilized by the collaborating team.

I built a friendship relationship with children and engaged them as a therapy dog owner and their friend in talking and writing about how Carmel teaches them to be kind. I then used my book to engage them in activities such as visualizing and eventually engaged children in writing their own autobiographies. Simply, I read parts of my own book, "From unruly to therapy dog: The amazing journey" (Vokatis, 2021) and asked children to visualize certain scenes and then describe the visualizations as well as write them down and illustrate. In this way, children saw me as a reader, writer and a publishing author besides being a class friend who brings her dog in. Our friendship served as a springboard to introducing other aspects of my life regarding Carmel, such as writing and publishing about my dog.

It is also very important that the teacher and therapy dog owner are devoted to working together throughout these activities, both during dog therapy sessions and in weekly meetings, in order to reflect on how the activity is going and what needs to be changed, as well as what the next steps are.

As we observed in our therapy-literacy lab, children saw me and Lucinda as a team. When I was engaging children in activities and thus taking the center stage, Lucinda was mostly helping children. When children were working on their own, both of us walked around and provided assistance based on children's needs. Children saw us as partners and friends working together. They also saw a connection beyond our working in the classroom as they knew Lucinda also appeared in one of my books. In addition, both Lucinda and I are enthusiastic individuals who use imagination and playfulness. For instance, when we saw that Carmel wagged her tail when the child gave an answer, we imagined that this action symbolized Carmel's confirmation and we would say to the child with enthusiasm: "Did you see how Carmel wags her tail? That means she confirms your answer is correct!"

Virtual weekly meetings with Lucinda were very instrumental in ensuring the continuity of activities. Lucinda and I always started with reflecting on how a particular activity went. Throughout the process, we also tried to conceptualize what was happening in terms of the nature of children's relationship with Carmel, and decided on what we should work on next as a team in response to children's interest and engagement. In these discussions, we always shared ideas in organic, friendly, and respectful ways. I remember that in each discussion, we were always excited about what we noticed happening in the classroom and equally excited about the potential of our new ideas we developed together, shared, and agreed on.

LITERACY/DOG THERAPY LAB IN DIVERSE CLASSROOMS AND ACROSS CONTENT AREAS

The lessons provided and discussed here can be also differentiated based on different kinds of classrooms, like a special education classroom or a resource room with autistic children. As a matter of fact, the classroom where I taught with Lucinda had children who needed additional guidance and support to be successful. This type of therapy would positively influence children (even a resource room consisting of only children with autism disorder) and motivate them for writing. That is because contact with the dog diverts from negative behavior, promotes speech in nonverbal children, and builds confidence (Baird et al., 2022). Marcia, Emily, and Erica discuss their thoughts about this type of differentiation in our interview at the end of the book.

When it comes to using a similar approach in middle and high school, the most important aspect would be to start by visiting with the dog first to provide comfort, calmness, and joy. Then, it would be important to see how what the therapy dog owner writes or writes in collaboration with the teacher can possibly inspire middle and high school students. We would like to avoid prescribing anything specific here. Just like our activities developed organically and in response to children's needs and interests, we recommend a similar approach at the upper grade levels.

We also see a lot of potential in implementing dog therapy across content areas. As Lucinda and I continued to collaborate, we began incorporating math into Carmel's visits. Children learning how to count can use Carmel's kibble to perform addition and subtraction calculations. We can also think about science and social studies. As children are always curious about dogs, their questions can start an inquiry into dog breeds, genetics, and many other topics related to dogs or pets.

BARBARA VOKATIS' JOURNEY TO DOG THERAPY

Carmel and Barbara in Lucinda's math classroom in 2022

I am an associate professor who teaches undergraduate and graduate courses related to literacy. In addition, I have a certified therapy dog and I self-published about the benefits of dog therapy.

TEACHERS AND DOG THERAPY TEAMS

My journey to dog therapy visits started when my golden doodle, Carmel, was about six months old and I was not able to take her for a walk due to her extraordinary strength. Both regular collars and harnesses did not work, and only seemed to make the issue more challenging. As a result, I had to contact a local dog trainer and request help. As we began the training for the purpose of obedience and better walking on leash, the trainer saw some incredible potential in my dog's disposition and skills. That is how we decided to devote more time to training, particularly in the direction of pet therapy. In my book, "From unruly to therapy dog: The amazing journey," I describe more details of this journey.

June 2018 was a memorable month because Carmel and I passed a therapy dog test and became a therapy dog team. Starting in September of 2018, we began visiting a local school. Children immediately fell in love with Carmel and her calm but fun personality. Based on my observations and teachers' observations, the presence of Carmel gave them a sense of calmness, joy, relaxation, fun, confidence, and focus. I describe specific benefits of our dog therapy in that school and in those particular classrooms in my second book, "The amazing power of the dog therapy: How my therapy dog transformed children's learning."

When we visited the elementary school, we went to classrooms where children were learning different subjects. I would walk around with Carmel and stop at every desk so each child could pet her. This arrangement worked very well as the whole class could interact with her. I always saw children's and teachers' faces looking much happier when we came in and when they could touch Carmel. Teachers also told me that even a more challenging class turned into a very focused group when Carmel was visiting.

In particular, at the elementary level, I collaborated closely with one amazing teacher, Lucinda. I will never forget when she approached me in the school hallway and simply asked me who I was and what exactly I was doing with my dog in school. During this little conversation we made an arrangement that I was to go to her classroom the following week. This moment felt so special. It felt like she and I became instant friends and partners. Lucinda's openness, friendship, positive energy, love for both children and dogs, and curiosity with regards to what therapy dogs can do for children in her classrooms allowed us to sustain our visits when they went virtual during the COVID-19 pandemic. At the same time, her wonderful personality allowed us to work closely and creatively to come up with innovative teaching ideas incorporating dog therapy when in person therapy visits resumed.

In high school, we worked with a small group of special education students, and our visits worked a bit differently. We found that rewarding one or two children every week by allowing them to walk Carmel with my assistance was quite beneficial and gave them a sense of responsibility. Thanks to my gentle dog, one girl even overcame her fear of dogs as she slowly learned to pet Carmel.

In fact, even when COVID-19 interrupted our in-person visits, we continued them creatively online and still were able to provide valuable experiences for children and their parents. But the 2021-2022 school year was undoubtedly special, as Lucinda and I began coming up with new ideas in order to sharpen our dog therapy activities to strengthen second graders' literacy achievement. When I recollect our virtual meetings in the school year of 2021-2022, they were always full of enthusiasm and admiration of what we both observed as beneficial and making a huge change for children.

LUCINDA ORMISTON'S JOURNEY TO CLASSROOM WITH DOG THERAPY

Carmel and Lucinda in 2022

I am a native of Upstate New York and a second grade/Response to Intervention Math in Upstate New York.

My journey working with the wonderful Barb started on the day I saw her walking down the hall in our elementary school. Due to my love for animals, I was intrigued each time I saw Barb and Carmel walk past my classroom and kept saying to myself that I should ask her what she was doing in our school. At the time, I was teaching third grade. One day I saw Barb and Carmel walk by my room and said to myself, "I am going to stop her and see why they are here." That was the day I started my beautiful journey with Barb and Carmel.

I went into the hall and asked, "Why do you visit all the time?" Barb turned around and couldn't be any sweeter. She said, "Hi, I am Barb and this is Carmel. Carmel and I are a therapy dog team." I introduced myself and told her I love animals and would like her and Carmel to be involved with my class. Barb agreed right away. That was one of the best days of my life for myself and for the children in my classroom. We hit it off and became not only friends but a therapy dog classroom team.

As I reflect on Carmel, Barbara, and our journey working with my students, I remember what life was like before COVID-19 hit our country. Let me reflect briefly on my classroom and the journey. When entering my classroom, you would see my beautiful class in groups and enjoying sitting together in their learning environment. Carmel and Barbara joined us frequently and my kids loved it! The joy in their faces said it all. As I was teaching, Barbara would walk around and allow the children to pet and snuggle up to Carmel. It eased the children when they would come in.

One particular time, I distinctly remember is when a little boy - I'll call him Joey - wouldn't show any emotion, or talk much. This continued for several weeks until one day while I was teaching, Carmel was visiting Joey's group of children. Carmel pushed her cute little nose against Joey as if to say, "Hey, why don't you pet me or tell me what you're thinking?" The next thing I saw was Joey bending over and talking in a whisper to Carmel. I heard him say, "I love you, Carmel. I love it when you come to see me." This melted my heart.

I knew this would help to open Joey up. Guess what? It did! Barb's heart melted too when I shared Joey's story with her. We knew this was the beginning of something big as a therapy dog team. That's when we started to discuss what more we could do in the classroom. The excitement between us was building at the thought of what was happening when Carmel entered my classroom.

Then March 13, 2020 happened. This was the day all our faculty and staff were asked to attend an important meeting in our auditorium. We were told that there was a strong possibility that the school would be closed due to COVID-19, and we would have to teach from home. Little did I know that pretty much our whole country would be shut down and the educational system would change to something we as educators hadn't ever seen before. We would be teaching virtually! What was happening? How would Barbara and Carmel be part of my classroom? This was a scary time and my students and their families were anxious.

Many things were running through my head, but I knew that it was necessary for Barbara and Carmel to be part of our virtual experience. After a few weeks of getting things set up, kids online, Barbara and I came up with a plan. We knew we had to figure out how we could get them into the virtual classroom. We knew the importance of it at this critical time with the kids being isolated at home. We did it! We selected a time for the visits, and I told the class that I had a great big surprise for them.

Well, the day came that the children were going to get their big surprise. After several weeks of the children doing the best they could to continue their learning, the surprise was about to happen. I shared my screen with my class, and there was Barb and Carmel! The kids were shocked and so happy. I heard comments such as, "It's Carmel and Mrs. V. They are here with us!" The joy in the children's eyes was unforgettable. There was a sense of calm in each of them.

We explained to the children that Carmel and Mrs. V. were going to visit weekly to help them feel more at ease while learning. For the remainder of this school year, Carmel and Barbara visited so the kids could still see them and ask questions, no matter what they were. They ranged from how Barb and Carmel were feeling to questions about therapy dogs. It was amazing to say the least. I saw so many benefits to Carmel and Barbara's visits. The children seemed so much more relaxed when Carmel and Barbara visited. The children didn't want to miss any virtual classes because they didn't want to miss the opportunity to see Carmel and Barbara. They knew these visits meant there was time to talk about their feelings or ask questions related to how Carmel became a therapy dog. This intrigued Barbara and me. We decided that if virtual learning was going to occur in the next school year, it would be essential to have both of them join our class once or twice a week to help the children.

In August 2020, I was assigned to be the only virtual teacher for the second grade. I previously was a third grade teacher. I was now in a new grade level, new curriculum, 19 new virtual students, and had to set my classroom up to teach virtual for the whole school year. Barbara and I came up with a plan to integrate me, her and Carmel as a therapy team. This was exciting! We knew the children would love it and get great benefits from it. We knew this therapy team approach was going to have a permanent impact on my class.

We started slowly, with simple visits and short conversations. As the year went on, the kids would ask me, "When is Carmel and Mrs. V. coming to our class?" Although they knew the set dates, they wanted more visits. Barb and I started to discuss what topics we could talk about during our visits. The children wanted to know everything from how Carmel became a therapy dog to what treats Carmel liked. It was fascinating to hear what the students were curious about, and what they learned from the classroom conversations. There was a set of twins in my class that had a hummingbird land in one of their hands. They wanted to share this experience and the photo with Carmel and Barb. Other students started sharing when they were sad or happy with Carmel. It was so fascinating to hear and see the children opening up to Carmel like this.

This continued throughout the year, until one day I was told that Carmel and Barbara could visit the children in person, but only outside the school, under a big white tent that was set up for the children to take mask breaks. I reached out to the parents of my children and gave them a date to meet us. This was amazing! The children could meet Mrs. V. and Carmel in person. The excitement was unreal.

The day came to meet and the children were so excited. Many were very nervous, as you can imagine, due to Covid-19. Soon though, Carmel was walking around with Barbara to see the children. The children couldn't control their excitement. They wanted to hug and pet Carmel. Pictures were taken, along with many questions for Carmel and Mrs. V. Barbara and I saw the joy and excitement in the children's faces. We knew even more that therapy teams were crucial to children in the classroom. When the school year ended, we were still working around the pandemic.

The 2021 - 2022 school year came around. I would again be teaching second grade. I knew part of my curriculum would have to involve Barbara and Carmel. Although the children were back in the classroom, it was still going to be difficult due to the children having to be six feet apart, wearing masks, and not being able to sit or work in groups. Barbara and I were determined to get my class excited about being back and writing.

It started with weekly visits from Barb and Carmel. The joy in the children's faces was beautiful. Barbara and I decided we would incorporate her visits into the curriculum I was teaching. It worked even better than we expected! What we thought would start as a conversation, led us to having each student write their own autobiography. The excitement and enthusiasm from the children was unbelievable. Before Carmel and Barb started visiting, I had students who didn't like writing and didn't want to do any kind of writing at all! I couldn't get a few of my students to even speak in class. This all changed when Barb, Carmel, and I told the children they would be writing their very own autobiography.

Each step in the process took several weeks to complete. But the children didn't care what it took to complete. They listened to Barbara as we worked with the children on each step of the writing process. Barbara shared the books she had written and published to help explain the steps of writing a book. The children listened with enthusiasm and followed along.

I distinctly remember one of my students who didn't like writing and barely ever spoke. One day he said, "Ms. O., I love writing now. I want to write another book when I'm done with this one." Let me tell you, I almost started crying. We did it! Barbara and I, along with Carmel's love, helped this student come out of his shell. We found that with our teamwork, he actually realized he loved writing. It was a very special day for both of us.

Each time Barbara and Carmel came to my classroom, the kids didn't want them to leave. The time would go so fast when they visited. They became part of our classroom family. Often, I heard the children say, "Mrs. V., why can't you and Carmel stay with Ms. O. and us so we can keep writing more?" The excitement I saw in Barbara's face was precious. At this point in our work together, we knew we had excelled in what we originally set out to do. We discussed this in one of our meetings. We talked about how we went beyond what we thought we were going to accomplish.

We were, and still are, very excited about our therapy teamwork with Carmel.

The 2022/2023 school year, I worked as a math specialist for the elementary school. Barbara and I successfully incorporated our therapy teamwork in a smaller setting and for math.

When I think back to the time when I didn't have Barbara and Carmel visiting my classroom, I think about the children that Carmel could have helped that were shy, sad, or struggled at home. Barbara's ray of sunshine and Carmel's sweet love for children have been such a positive thing in my years of working with them. It makes me think that in the future I would like to train a dog to be a permanent part of my classrooms.

If I could give one word of advice, I would say that if you have never tried having a therapy dog team, it's time. You'll be amazed at what occurs with the children in your classroom.

THE PATHWAY TO THE LITERACY/THERAPY DOG LAB

Drawing created by one of Lucinda's students in 2022

Following successful visits in Lucinda's classrooms before COVID-19 and virtually, Carmel and I started dog visits to Lucinda's second grade classroom in September 2021. As we began visiting, we formed a friendship between our therapy team and the children. The children developed a friendly relationship with me as a result of my attitude and my interactions with them. When children interacted with my dog in class, I often smiled at them. In response to me, they reciprocated with their smiles and often shared their feelings and emotions they experienced when they touched Carmel. I heard reactions such as: "Carmel is so soft," "Carmel is the best dog," or "I love Carmel so much!" I always responded to these reactions by saying "Thank you so much," or "Carmel also loves you."

In a way, I was my dog's spokesperson and this communication extended children's interaction with Carmel. Children's attachment became an attachment to both of us as a team, not just to Carmel. I realized the scale of this attachment during many touching moments in the classroom, such as children hugging me as I was leaving with Carmel at the end of each session.

As Carmel was becoming an integral part of Lucinda's classroom community, both Lucinda and I started thinking about ways to incorporate these visits into Lucinda's curriculum. That is how the idea of the therapy dog/literacy lab was born. It came about very spontaneously and organically, out of the need to help this specific class of lively children become more focused. They were eager to learn about my therapy dog and experience the love my dog was giving them. Right from the beginning, we intertwined a therapy/community building aspect with literacy, albeit in very simple ways at first.

First, I had wonderful conversations with children, when I could answer their questions and listen to their sharing about their own animals. I also saw Lucinda interacting with Carmel and inviting children to interact as well. She allowed them to leave their desks and interact with my dog in respectful ways, such as petting her gently, and not pulling on her tail. I saw children growing their great attachment as they were telling me they love Carmel. I saw that every child wanted to make sure he or she would never miss an opportunity to pet her.

I noticed that something extremely touching was happening. Children did not just pet Carmel. They wanted to experience her softness and warmth on their cheeks. Therefore, they experimented with touching her and I could see the relaxed expression on their faces when they did. In addition, I saw children's kindness and attachment towards me as they were asking me how I was doing and giving me pieces of paper with hearts they drew. As we were becoming a true community, right at the beginning, we asked children to write about what Carmel's visits did for them. This simple prompt gave them a very authentic reason to write.

We found out from their writings that Carmel made the children very happy and calmed them. Writing about anything in connection to Carmel gave the children even more joy by the act of putting words on paper. Therefore, after Lucinda's return from a leave, we started thinking about other ways of incorporating Carmel's visits into children's writing, which persuaded many students to become lifelong authors. In an interview, Lucinda said, "I have had some of the kids say 'I want to be a writer when I get older.' That's awesome. I can picture some of these kids when they are 25-30 years old. They come back and say 'I can remember in second grade working with Mrs. V and Carmel and that's what sparked my interest in writing.'"

During that time, it also became obvious to me that I was not just a certified therapy dog owner. I became more of a participant because my task was no longer to only handle my dog during the therapy, but to also work with the teacher and students as we incorporated concrete educational activities into the curriculum.

In March, one of the school's themes was kindness. We agreed that as a therapy dog owner, I could lead the children into thinking what they can learn about kindness from Carmel and then have them write about what they learned. Children not only had wonderful answers and a lot of thoughts concerning how Carmel shows kindness, but each child also had a very original answer. For instance, one child said that she would hug her family members just like Carmel likes to be hugged. Another child said she would help a family member if they needed help just like Carmel helps others.

We then thought about using the book I wrote about Carmel to teach children about visualization. Visualization is a strategy of creating a picture or movie in the mind when reading a part of the story (Mackey, 2019). Visualization improves comprehension of the text because when the reader thinks of a picture or movie, it makes understanding of the text easier and engaging.

This idea was successful because it connected very well with the children. This made visualization more embedded in what the children already knew. They were so interested in details from Carmel's journey through puppyhood. When I asked the students to close their eyes and visualize a scene, their descriptions were so rich and went beyond the details I read to them from the book. Lucinda was impressed as well. In an interview, she said that her students liked to visualize Carmel as a "superhero dog. You know what I mean? She has super powers that help us learn."

I was so impressed that I told them that they should be authors themselves since they were essentially helping me to revise my book.

I was also deeply impressed with children's subsequent creative visualizations that often went beyond realistic happenings. The children visualized Carmel doing activities that were sometimes a fantasy, such as Carmel using a credit card in the store. That's because for them, Carmel was a special dog, a dog of several identities. As Lucinda says, "Carmel was a superhero dog for the children." Carmel was not just a therapist, comforting students. She also modeled good behavior for them. The children often spoke about how Carmel made them be more patient or pay more attention.

She was also an entertainer, a dog that would poke the child with her nose or try to snatch a stuffed animal. The children always stressed the fun aspect of interacting with her. Therefore, when the children were coming up with their visualization ideas, they saw Carmel as a dog capable of doing many things, beyond what dogs can do. Lucinda also noticed something very striking. Each child really wanted to create his or her own idea and share, which was in contrast to many children's usual response such as "I have the same idea." The children wanted to contribute their own, original ideas. Each child was comfortable and eager to be a part of this sharing within the therapy dog classroom community. In an interview conducted at the end of an autobiography unit based on Carmel, a boy named John even said, "My favorite part was playing with her and getting to write books. When I get older, I'm going to write a couple thousand books."

When I heard the children's creative responses, I gave them a lot of praise and said that if I was writing my book now, it would be better because their responses would make my writing better. When I told the children their visualizations would improve my book and that they themselves can be authors, I literally saw children's faces showing me that they believe they could do it.

Children also were very interested in my book publishing experience. I shared some of these experiences with them, as well as told them they can be book authors just like I was. As the idea of book writing was coming from me as their friend, they felt comfortable and confident that they can also write a book. Since I, their friend, was telling them they can do it, they eagerly believed it and were very excited about the idea. When interviewed, a little girl named Katie even said "I always wanted to write a real book about something, and you gave me the opportunity."

The students also admired the fact that their teacher was included in my second book. They considered Lucinda, their teacher, a famous person because she appeared in my book. Both of us also started hearing more and more voices from the children that they want to be book authors. In another interview with Lucinda's class, Claire even said her favorite part about me visiting was writing "the books because I always wanted to write one. Then I got to write one."

Did we realize how big an impact having Carmel in the classroom would have on the children? No, we did not. But we saw that children were interested in anything initiated by me because of their already developed attachment to me and Carmel (Beck & Madresh, 2008). At one point, when we decided do just a regular therapy session with Carmel, which had no literacy activities, children actually said, "We want to do visualization!" This was such a crucial point because the fact that children demanded this literacy activity when Carmel and I were in the classroom meant that our organic lab idea was working very well.

When we asked children if they would like to write their own autobiographies, they all responded with great enthusiasm. As part of the interview, another little girl in Lucinda's class named Krista said,

"We get to write books and talk about books. We also get to illustrate in many different ways!"

Each subsequent lesson, such as creating a book cover, introduction, and writing the chapters were all met with continuous enthusiasm from the children. In fact, as Lucinda said to me, all children wanted to do is write, work on their autobiographies, and nothing else mattered to them. I personally witnessed this enthusiasm throughout my time spent in the classroom. As I was leaving the classroom, the children always asked me to stay longer with Carmel. This result is especially astonishing because the work on autobiographies was quite involved, consisting of many steps and also redoing the work for a final copy. In addition, we saw how children who would not even write a word became enthusiastic writers who wrote a book and had plans for writing more.

Moreover, as their work was finished, some children pledged that they would continue writing books during the summer. Some children decided they would become book writers and therapy dog handlers in the future. Children's responses to interview questions for my present research study were also striking. Some of these quotes are included in the above paragraphs. All children said that creating their own autobiographies and petting Carmel were the best parts of our therapy visits. As mentioned, a boy named John expressed his big life goal by announcing "When I get older, I'm going to write a couple thousand books!" In addition, when I returned to school for therapy visits after the summer, the children with whom we did these experimental activities welcomed Carmel and me by not only saying that they missed Carmel, but they also mentioned that they kept writing in the summer. Moreover, when I went to the school sensory carnival in April 2023, one of the boys who created his book in Lucinda's class approached me and told me that he came only because Carmel was going to be attending the carnival. He also mentioned that he still had the book. It was amazing to hear such wonderful words from the children. It was incredible that the children talked about writing and the books without me asking them about it.

OVERVIEW OF THE ACTIVITIES

In the next part of the book, we describe specific activities we developed and did with children. We would like to stress that it is important to start therapy dog visits without any literacy agenda in mind. It is extremely important that children experience the benefits of dog therapy the way they are intended, by simply interacting with the dog by petting, touching and gently rubbing the fur, etc. It's all about building the bond and letting children experience the closeness of the dog. During this time, the therapy dog owner should be more of a dog handler who observes interactions between the dog and the children.

It is also important that the owner shows a happy demeanor in interactions with children and be genuinely interested in what they say about their experiences from interacting with the dog. I heard children telling me things like, "Your dog is so soft," and "I love Carmel!" These are opportunities for the therapy dog owner to pay attention to children's reactions and build friendships with children. Each time I heard such reactions from children, I always responded by saying something like this: "Thank you. Carmel really loves you." However, it is perfectly fine to do some very simple activities such as asking children to write a couple of sentences about how the dog makes them feel and illustrate these feelings.

In addition, the activities we include here are only suggestions. They can be utilized, modified, used as inspiration, or completely different activities can be developed. The dynamics and characteristics of particular children's needs and interests should be the driving factor helping the teacher and therapy team decide what to pursue. Even the type of book the therapy dog owner decides to write can influence writing activities. My memoir was similar to an autobiography and that's what the children wrote. But a different genre (for example, a narrative picture book with a dialogue between characters) can lead children to writing a similar book. What really matters is the therapy dog owner's authentic love of reading and sharing it with children.

We hope that math activities and connecting math to social studies will inspire you to experiment with math teaching and learning that works best for a particular group of children. There are simply so many possibilities here. That's why observing children is so important and writing those observations. Weekly meetings between the teacher and the therapy dog owner will help you to reflect on the activities and decide what's next.

Please note that the writing activities were developed for the whole class while the math activities were taught in a small remedial math group.

WRITING ACTIVITIES

KINDNESS

Goal/Overview:

The main goal of this activity is to make the concept of kindness more tangible to children by asking them to describe how their therapy dog shows kindness, and also to teach them how to apply kindness displayed by the animal to their own circumstances as humans.

Pre-activity:

The teacher has a classroom activity prior to the therapy visit in which she explains to children what kindness means.

The dog therapy owner/activity participant thinks of asking children questions that are more open ended, which means inviting a variety of answers from children, not yes or no answers or correct answers. Specific questions can be found in the activity.

Activity:

- Children have some time with the therapy dog for petting.
- The therapy dog handler/activity participant engages the entire class by asking the following question: "How does your therapy dog show that he/she is a kind dog?" Other questions

can offer further support in case children need more help: "What exactly does your therapy dog do that shows he/she is kind?" "What does your therapy dog do in the classroom to show you he/she is a kind dog?"
- Children come up with their descriptions of therapy dog's kind behavior.
- The handler can say the following statement in order to connect these descriptions to how children can show kindness, "Think about how you can learn from the therapy dog about kindness. How can you show kindness to others? Remember, also, that not everything your therapy dog does can be followed as he/she is a dog and you are a person. You cannot, or should not, do everything the therapy dog does."
- Children come up with their ideas about how they can show kindness to other children, relatives, and animals.

Writing expression:

- Children respond to the following prompt: "What does kindness mean to you and what did you learn from your therapy dog about kindness?" They can also add a picture showing an act of kindness.
- This prompt can be assigned by the teacher after the therapy visit is over.

Extension:

Many other concepts similar to kindness can be taught in this way, such as inclusion, confidence, resilience, respect, etc. For instance, in the case of inclusion, a question for children might be: "How does your therapy dog show he/she includes everyone?" After children describe how their dog shows inclusion, the next question can be: "Think about how you can learn from the therapy dog about including others. How can you show inclusion to others? Remember, also, that not everything your therapy dog does can be followed as he/she is a dog and you are a person. You cannot, or should not, do everything the therapy dog does."

VISUALIZATION

Goal/Overview:

The main goal of this activity is to make the concept of visualization more understandable and relatable to children, as well as more engaging.

Concept:

Visualization is a process of creating a picture or movie in the mind when reading part of a story. Visualization improves comprehension of the text because when the reader thinks of a picture or movie, it makes the text easier to understand and more engaging.

Preparation:

Before this activity, the team should select a picture book. The best picture book for this activity would be one that has scenes suitable for visualizing. A story about a therapy dog would be appropriate and if the therapy dog owner has written one, even better. For our activity, we used my own book "From unruly to therapy dog: The amazing journey." If the teacher does not have access to a book about a dog, other books about kindness, compassion, friendship, etc. can be used.

Pre-activity:

The teacher has a classroom activity prior to the therapy visit in which she explains to children what visualization means.

Activity:

- Children have some time with the therapy dog for petting.
- The therapy dog owner/activity participant engages the whole class by asking the following question, "What do you know about visualization?" Other questions can offer further support in case children need more help: "What does it mean to visualize?" Children might answer that visualizing means creating a picture in their mind as they read a scene from a book. It can be also added that creating a movie in their mind can also help in their visualizing.
- The therapy dog owner/activity participant does a short book introduction by showing the book cover and, if written by the owner, discussing the inspiration for the book. If the book is written by someone else, the therapy dog owner/activity participant can say something different. For instance, he or she can say, "What inspired that author to write the book?"
- The therapy dog owner/activity participant explains to children: "I will read first. When we come to the part, I want you to visualize, I will ask you to close your eyes."
- The therapy dog owner/activity participant reads and asks children to visualize certain scenes. Each time they visualize, they share their visualizations.

Drawing and Writing Expression:

- Children draw their visualizations and then describe them in writing. This activity takes place after the therapy team leaves.

Drawing created by one of Lucinda's students in 2022

BIOGRAPHY/AUTOBIOGRAPHY/MEMOIR

Goal/Overview:

The main goal of this activity is to make the concepts of biography / autobiography / memoir more understandable and relatable to children, as well as more engaging.

Concepts:

A biography is a life story written by someone else, not the person featured in the life story. An autobiography is a life story written by the person featured in the story. A memoir is a collection of memories written by the person themselves.

Preparation:

Before this activity, the team should select a picture book. The best picture book for this activity would be one that is an autobiography with a dedication and introduction. For our activity, we used my own book, "From unruly to therapy dog: The amazing journey." However, one might also use a different book. It could be a book about any dog written in the form of a memoir and connections to the therapy dog can be made by the reader when reading it to the children. If a book like this is not available, any memoir with a dedication will work as well. If the collaborating team chooses a different book genre that is not a biography, the conversation with children will be different. For instance, instead of asking children what a biography is, the therapy dog owner can ask children what a story is.

Pre-activity:

The teacher has a classroom activity prior to the therapy visit in which she explains to children what a biography / autobiography / memoir is.

Activity:

- Children have some time with the therapy dog for petting.
- The therapy dog owner/activity participant engages the whole class by asking the following question, "What do you know about a biography?" Other questions can offer further support in case children need more help: "What is a biography?"
- The next concept to discuss is an autobiography, with a question such as, "What is an autobiography?" "What do you think?" "How is a biography different from an autobiography?" For older students, in grade 4 and up, the following questions can be asked: "Do you notice what the words *Bio*, *Biography* and *Autobiography* have in common?"
- The next concept to discuss is a memoir, with a question such as, "What is a memoir?" and "How is a memoir different from a biography and an autobiography?"
- The therapy dog owner/activity participant can finish this activity by reading other parts of the book and asking children to visualize.

Drawing and Writing Expression:

- Children draw their visualizations and then describe them in writing. This activity takes place after the therapy team leaves.

BOOK COVER

Goal/Overview:

The main goal of this activity is to brainstorm ideas about what makes a book cover good.

Concepts:

The overarching rule is that the book cover has to be beautiful and has to go with the plot, characters, and/or theme of the book.

Other things to consider:

1. Gather book cover design inspiration
2. Outline the book's main themes
3. Consider the genre
4. Get rid of the clutter
5. Choose appropriate fonts and colors
6. Make your title stand out
7. Don't overlook the spine or back cover

Preparation:

Before this activity, the team should select a picture book. If children write a biography or autobiography, the best picture book for this activity would be one that is an autobiography. A memoir written by the therapy dog owner/activity participant is even better. The book should have a dedication and introduction. For our activity, we used my book, "From unruly to therapy dog: The amazing journey." However, one might also use a biography or memoir about another dog. If children write a different genre, such as a story, a different book will be used as an example.

Activity:

- Children have some time with the therapy dog for petting.
- The therapy dog owner/activity participant engages the whole class by asking the following question, "When you look at the book cover of the book I wrote, what do you notice about it?" "What makes a good book cover?" "What do you notice about the pictures and title?"
- The therapy dog owner/activity participant then reminds children that it is very important that the book cover is beautiful and reflects what the book is about.
- The therapy dog owner/activity participant then tells children: "Your autobiography can be just general about your life, your family, and pets. But you can also write about how your hobbies developed, or what happened across all your school grades." Then, the therapy dog owner/activity participant asks children: "What is your idea about your autobiography?" "What is your autobiography title?" All children share their ideas.

Drawing and Writing Expression:

- Children compose their book covers. This activity takes place after the therapy team leaves.

DEDICATION AND INTRODUCTION

Goal/Overview:

The main goal of this activity is to explain to children the role of a dedication and introduction, model both sections, and have them write their original ones.

Concepts:

A dedication is a short statement in which a book author dedicates his or her book to someone else. An introduction is a short section at the beginning of the book to grab readers' attention.

Preparation:

Before this activity, the team should select a picture book. The best picture book for this activity would be one that is an autobiography or memoir with a dedication and introduction. A memoir written by the therapy dog owner/activity participant is even better. For our activity, we used my book, "From unruly to therapy dog: The amazing journey." However, one might also use a book about another dog. If children write a different genre, such as a story, a different book will be used as an example.

Pre-activity:

The teacher has a classroom activity prior to the therapy visit. During this time the children create the final versions of their autobiography covers if they were not done earlier.

Activity:

- Children have some time with the therapy dog for petting.
- The therapy dog owner/activity participant engages the whole class by reading her own book dedication and asking the following question, "What do you notice about my dedication?"
- She then asks children to come up with their own ideas about dedications.
- The next concept to discuss is an introduction. The therapy dog owner/activity participant reads her own introduction and asks children what they notice about how she tried to grab the reader's attention. Then, she asks them to write their own introductions.
- If some children have a harder time with this writing, the teacher can write a model introduction and display it for them to copy or modify.

Drawing and Writing Expression:

- Children compose their book introductions and dedications. This activity takes place after the therapy team leaves.

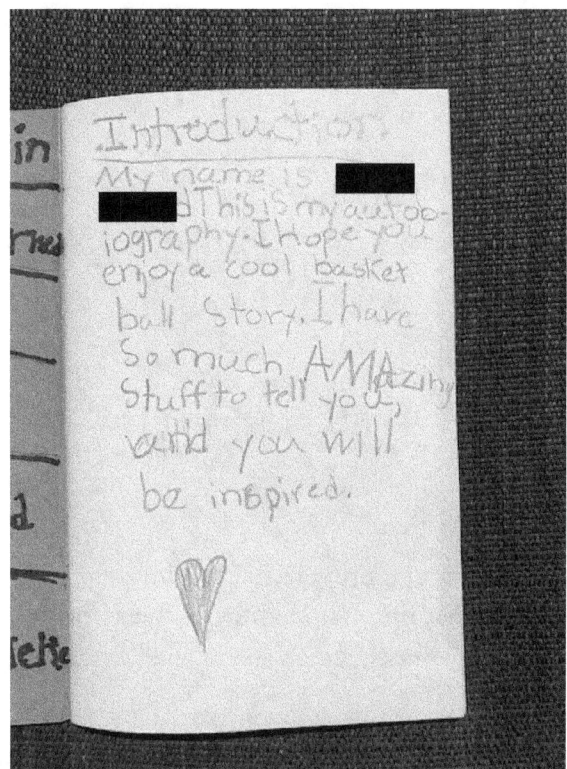

Book introduction written by one of the children who created autobiographies in Lucinda's classroom in 2022

FIRST CHAPTER

Goal/Overview:

The main goal of this activity is to help children in brainstorming ideas about the content for the first chapter of their books.

Preparation:

Before this activity, the team should select a picture book. The best picture book for this activity would be one that is an autobiography or memoir. A memoir written by the therapy dog owner/activity participant is even better. For our activity, we used my book, "From unruly to therapy dog: The amazing journey." However, one might also use a book about another dog. If children write a different genre, such as a story, a different book will be used as an example.

Pre-activity:

The teacher has a classroom activity prior to the therapy visit in which children create the final versions of their autobiography dedications and introductions if they were not done earlier.

Activity:

- Children have some time with the therapy dog for petting.
- The therapy dog owner/activity participant engages the whole

class by reading her own first chapter from the book and asking the following question, "What do you notice about my first chapter and its title?"
- She then asks children to come up with their own ideas about their first chapters.
- If some children have a harder time with this writing, the teacher can write a model chapter and display for them to copy or modify.

Drawing and Writing Expression:

- Children compose their first book chapter. This activity takes place after the therapy team leaves.

AUTHOR'S BIO FOR BACK COVER

Goal/Overview:

The main goal of this activity is to help children in brainstorming ideas about the bios for their back book covers.

Preparation:

Before this activity, the team should select a picture book. The best picture book for this activity would be one that is an autobiography or memoir. A memoir written by the therapy dog owner/activity participant is even better. For our activity, we used my book, "From unruly to therapy dog: The amazing journey." However, one might also use a book about another dog. If children write a different genre, such as a story, a different book will be used as an example.

Pre-activity:

The teacher has a classroom activity prior to the therapy visit in which children write more chapters for their books.

Activity:

- Children have some time with the therapy dog for petting.
- The therapy dog owner/activity participant engages the whole class by reading her own bio and asking the following

question, "What do you notice about my author's bio?"
- She then asks children to come up with their own ideas about their bios, such as including their name, grade level, interests, and life goals.
- If some children have a harder time with this writing, the teacher can write an example chapter and display for them to copy or modify.

Drawing and Writing Expression:

- Children compose their own bios. This activity takes place after the therapy team leaves.

When their rough drafts are created, children should create the final copies of their books. The final copies can be created when the therapy team is with the children or after the therapy team leaves. In our case, the children did some of this work when Carmel and I were in the classroom.

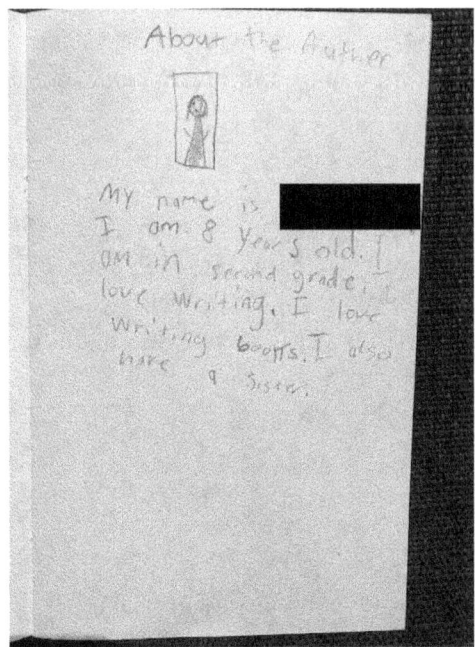

Author's bio written by one of Lucinda's students who wrote autobiographies in 2022

MATH ACTIVITIES

PLACE VALUE

Goal/Overview:

The main goal of this activity is to make the concept of place value in math more understandable and relatable to children, as well as more engaging. Another goal is to also engage children in writing about it.

Concept:

Place value is an important concept in math. For instance, in the number 54, there are two types of place value. The place value of the digit 5 is in the tens place, and the place value of the digit 4 is ones place. It is important for students to understand that 5 does not mean 5 but actually 5 tens, with the value of 50. The 4 is in the ones place, which means it is 4 ones, with the value of 4. Five tens and four ones make 54.

Preparation:

Before this activity, the team should get together and discuss how this concept will be taught with the help of the therapy dog.

Pre-activity:

The teacher has a classroom activity prior to the therapy visit in which she explains and teaches to children about place value. This is also an opportunity to see what children have a harder time understanding. In our case, the teacher noticed the children could not understand that 5 in 54 stands for 50 and kept saying it is just 5.

Activity:

- Children have some time with the therapy dog for petting.
- The therapy dog owner/activity participant engages the whole class or group of children by asking them what facts they know about the therapy dog, such as her breed and age, but focuses on weight, asking children to estimate the dog's weight.
- Once the weight is estimated, the therapy dog owner/activity participant writes it on the white board and goes over its place values. If the weight is 65 pounds, the therapy dog owner/activity participant draws children's attention to the digit 6 asking them what that means. Children should respond that it is 6 tens, which is the value of 60. If they do not respond that it is 6 tens, the therapy dog owner should review with children that 6 stands for six tens and try with children again.
- The teacher gives students an activity in which they are asked to determine the place values in the number representing the weight of another dog.

Writing Expression:

- Children can be asked to write how the therapy dog helped them in understanding place value in math.

Extension:

- Talking about weight for different dogs is an opportunity to engage children in greater and less than activities.

ADDITION 1-12

Goal/Overview:

The main goal of this activity is to make addition more engaging for children and to also engage children in writing about it.

Preparation:

Before this activity, the team should get together and discuss how to incorporate the therapy dog to make addition more engaging for children. In this case, we decided to use my therapy dog's dry dog food. In this way, children would use the dry dog food to manipulate it for addition, thus engaging with it more as it is connected to the dog they love.

Pre-activity:

Prior to the activity, children practice 1-10 addition by rolling dice, using laminated tens frames to put tokens on them based on the outcome of dice rolling, and writing addition equations on the white board.

Activity:

- Children have some time with the therapy dog for petting.

- The teacher invites the therapy dog team to the activity by explaining it. Or, children can explain the activity to the therapy dog team. The teacher also tells children that for this activity they will be using therapy dog's dry dog food.
- Each student team engages with the activity by rolling a die twice and placing as many pieces of dog food as indicated by dice rolling. Children can also ask the therapy dog owner to roll the dice.
- Each student team writes their addition on the white board and places the dog food used in the manipulation in a special bowl for the dog to eat.

Writing Expression:

- Children can be asked to write what they liked about working on math with their therapy dog.

ADDITION 1-20

Goal/Overview:

The main goal of this activity is to make addition more engaging for children and to also engage children in writing about it.

Preparation:

Before this activity, the team should get together and discuss how to incorporate the therapy dog to make addition more engaging for children. In this case, we decided to use my therapy dog's dry dog food. In this way, children would use the dry dog food to manipulate it for addition, thus engaging with it more as it is connected to the dog.

Pre-activity:

Prior to the activity, children practiced 1-10 and 1-20 addition by rolling dice and putting tokens next to each other based on the outcome of dice rolling, and writing addition equations on the white board.

Activity:

- Children have some time with the therapy dog for petting.
- The teacher explains to children that they will use the therapy

dog's dog food to manipulate it for addition. In order to do it, they will sit in front of the white board, on the rug. Each child will have a plastic tray with a little dish that has dog food. After they are done with manipulation, the therapy dog will come to each child and eat the kibble from the tray.
- Each time the teacher assigns the addition, each student takes an appropriate number of dog food pieces from their dish and puts them on the tray.
- The teacher then announces that the therapy dog will be going around and will be checking if the additions are done correctly and will eat the kibble.
- After the activity, the trays are disinfected by the teacher.

Writing Expression:

- Children can be asked to write what they liked about working on math with their therapy dog.

ADDITION GAME WITH THE THERAPY DOG

Goal/Overview:

The main goal of this activity is to make addition more engaging for children and to also engage children in creative ideas and writing about it.

Preparation:

Before this activity, the team should get together and discuss how to incorporate the therapy dog to make addition more engaging for children by adding an additional aspect, playing a game with the therapy dog. In this case, we decided to use my therapy dog's dry dog food, as in previous lessons.

We decided to incorporate three plastic cups. After children use kibble for addition and do it correctly, their reward is to play a game with the therapy dog. For this game, children use three plastic cups. They put a certain amount of kibble under one cup and leave the other ones empty. Cups are put upside down so it's not visible which cup has dog food. Of course, they make sure the dog cannot see this preparation. Then, children tell the dog two numbers they added and invite the dog to guess which cup contains the kibble with the right answer.

Pre-activity:

Prior to the activity, children practiced 1-10 and 1-20 addition with the teacher.

Activity:

- Children have some time with the therapy dog for petting.
- The teacher explains to children that they will use therapy dog's dog food to manipulate it for addition. In order to do it, they will sit in front of the white board, on the rug. Each child will have a plastic tray with a little dish that has dog food. After they are done with addition manipulation assigned by the teacher, the therapy dog will come to each child and eat the kibble to indicate the addition was done correctly.
- Each time the teacher assigns the addition, each student takes an appropriate number of dog food pieces from their dish and puts them on the tray.
- The teacher then announces that the therapy dog will be going around to check if the addition problems are done correctly, and will eat the kibble.
- After the activity, the trays are disinfected by the teacher.
- As a reward for addition done well, the teacher asks children to choose an addition for the therapy dog for the game. One child tells the therapy dog a task such as 5 plus 7.
- The children and the teacher place 12 pieces of kibble under one of the plastic cups and leave the other ones empty. Everybody makes sure the dog does not see which cup has the kibble.
- Children invite the dog to come and find the cup with the dog food in it.
- The dog finds the kibble and eats it.

Writing Expression:

- The teacher asks the children to write their ideas for other activities/games with the dog.
- Our children came up with the hide and seek idea. If Carmel finds all hidden cups, with one of them containing a certain amount of kibble, it will mean she knows the answer.

SUBTRACTION 1-20

Goal/Overview:

The main goal of this activity is to make subtraction more engaging for children and to also engage children in writing about it.

Preparation:

Before this activity, the team should get together and discuss how to incorporate the therapy dog to make subtraction more engaging for children. In this case, we decided to use my therapy dog's dry dog food. In this way, children would use the dry dog food to manipulate it for subtraction, thus engaging with it more as it is connected to the dog.

Pre-activity:

Prior to the activity, children practiced 1-10 and 1-20 subtraction by rolling dice and putting tokens next to each other based on the outcome of dice rolling, and writing subtraction equations on the white board.

Activity:

- Children have some time with the therapy dog for petting.
- The teacher explains to children that they will use the therapy

dog's dog food to manipulate it for subtraction. In order to do it, they will sit in front of the white board, on the rug. Each child will have a plastic tray with a little dish that has dog food. After they are done with manipulation, the therapy dog will come to each child and eat the kibble.

- Each time the teacher assigns the subtraction, each student takes an appropriate number of dog food pieces from their dish, puts them on the tray, and then takes what is subtracted and puts it back into the dish.
- The teacher then announces that the therapy dog will be going around and checking if the subtraction problems are done correctly and will eat the kibble.
- After the activity, the trays are disinfected by the teacher.

Writing Expression:

- Children can be asked to write what they liked about working on math with their therapy dog.

ESTIMATION AND MAP SKILLS

Goal/Overview:

The main goal of this activity is to make estimating and learning map skills more engaging for children.

Preparation:

Before this activity, the team should get together and discuss how to incorporate the therapy dog to connect estimating with learning map skills.

Pre-activity:

Prior to the activity, children practiced addition and also learned some basic things about maps, such as what an inch on the map would mean in terms of miles. In addition, either the teacher or the therapy dog owner/activity participant prepares a little paper cutout of the therapy dog that can be used to move around on the map. If possible, the teacher can obtain a large piece of fabric and draw the basic world map on it, with some major cities.

Activity:

- Children have some time with the therapy dog for petting.
- The teacher, children, and the therapy dog team gather around

a map.
- The teacher explains to children that they will take turns and each child will place the cutout on a place of the child's choice, measure how many inches the cutout moved from the previous place, and estimate how many miles this distance would be. The teacher can also engage children in the discussion of the ways of transportation to the place of their choice.
- The teacher places the cutout on the map and asks the first child to place it on any place on the map, measure the distance in inches, and estimate the real distance in miles.
- Each child gets to do the same task.
- The therapy dog team chooses a spot on the map after all children did the activity.

Writing Expression:

- The teacher asks the children to write where they would like to take their therapy dog on a class trip in the area where they live.

BEGINNING FRACTIONS

Goal/Overview:

The main goal of this activity is to make understanding the concept of fractions more engaging for children.

Preparation:

Before this activity, the team should get together and discuss how to incorporate the therapy dog to connect learning the concept of fractions.

Pre-activity:

Prior to the activity, children had a lesson introducing them to fractions.

Activity:

- Children have some time with the therapy dog for petting.
- Every child gets a special dog treat and is asked to break it into two even pieces.
- The teacher or therapy dog owner/activity participant tells children that one piece is one part of the whole treat.
- Children are asked to give one part to the dog and are asked how much is left.

- The teacher or the therapy dog owner/activity participant writes the fraction ½ on the board and explains the connection between the treat and the fraction.

Writing Expression:

- The teacher asks the children to write how the therapy dog helped them in understanding fractions.

FINAL THOUGHTS

We hope that the activities we presented inspired teachers and therapy dog teams to work together and conduct something similar with children. The power of the circle of friendship (teacher - therapy dog team - children) is what started our amazing collaboration and resulted in some substantial benefits for the participating class of second graders and math groups. We would love to hear from you about your activities and children's responses to them.

Please contact the first author at:

Website: www.barbaravokatis.com
Instagram: https://www.instagram.com/dr.barb.educator
Facebook: https://www.facebook.com/barbara.vokatis

REVIEW THE BOOK

Dear Reader,

If this book resonated with you, we would appreciate your book review. Reviews are very helpful to authors. Thank you from advance.

HOW TO EASILY SELF-PUBLISH A BOOK

- Write a memoir that tells a story of your journey to becoming a certified therapy team.
- Show your draft to several people for revision and editing ideas.
- Pick photography you would like to include in your book.
  - Using your own photography will save a lot of your financial assets as illustrators charge a lot for illustrations.
- Find a freelance book designer who can do the following: design a book cover, format the book as both hard copy and ebook, guide you in setting up a publishing account on Amazon, help in uploading book files, and create promotional posts. I recommend choosing a book designer from the following platform: https://www.fiverr.com
  - In choosing a designer, consider how long they have been designing, their reviews, and their design samples.
  - Our designer is Shrikesh Kumar and we recommend him without a hesitation: https://www.fiverr.com/flamescreations. His price is affordable.
- Set up your account on Kindle Direct Publishing at https://kdp.amazon.com/en_US/

Alternatively, instead of doing it yourself, you can send a book proposal/manuscript of your book to a publisher. Going with a publisher will give you more support in terms of refining your manuscript. We recommend SchoolRubric (www.schoolrubric.org).

SOME BOOKS WITH THE THERAPY DOGS THEME

Title: Archer the Therapy Dog: A Read Together Book
Author: Katie Baron
Ages: 6-10 and also adults

>Archer, a lovable golden retriever, invites you and your child to join him on his journey as he becomes a therapy dog and makes visits to a library, a school, a nursing home, and a hospital.

Title: Augie the Therapy Doggie
Author: Heather Vina
Ages: 6-10

>It is a story written from the dog's perspective about how Augie becomes a therapy dog.

Title: Buster and the Brain Bully
Author: Christina Pellegrino
Ages: 6-10

>It is a story of Buster, a sweet golden retriever who battles anxiety but learns ways to deal with it so that he can become a therapy dog.

Title: Moxy Makes a Difference
Author: Nicole Selby & Tonya Cartmell
Ages: 6-10

>This is not only a great story about how a therapy dog can help someone overcome fears, but it's also a lesson in not judging someone by what they look like.

Title: Brisco, Life as a Therapy Dog
Author: Margot Bennett
Age: 10+

>This book is told from Brisco's point of view and tells a story of the bond between dogs and humans and how therapy dogs

contribute to that bond.

Title: May I Pet Your Dog?
Author: Stephanie Calmenson
Ages: 6-10

This book is great for visualization. It is about the proper way to approach a dog.

TEACHERS AND DOG THERAPY TEAMS

Permission Slip to Participate in Therapy Dog Visits (Example)

Dear Parents/Guardians:

Our school will be hosting therapy dog visits in partnership with Barbara Vokatis and Therapy Dogs International. This program includes trained, registered and certified NY State volunteer Barbara Vokatis and her adult dog who adheres to environmental health and safety policies. Participating dogs must be certified therapy dogs, have completed extensive classes in obedience, and be current on their immunizations. There is no charge for this program.

Participation by your child in this program will not begin until your written permission is received. You have the right to refuse participation in this program. At any time, you may terminate your participant's authorization to participate.

The school would not be responsible for any medical issues perceived to be secondary to exposure to the therapy dog. The school does not anticipate any problems with this.

In addition to signing below, please indicate (by circling either Yes or No), whether your participant is allergic to dogs or other animals. In the interest of your participant's safety, if your participant is allergic, we cannot offer participation in the program.

TEACHERS AND DOG THERAPY TEAMS

Screening questions:

My participant is afraid of dogs.	Yes	No
My participant is allergic to animals.	Yes	No
My participant has an autoimmune disease.	Yes	No
My participant has been diagnosed with a medical condition that may compromise is/her health if he/she is in close proximity to a dog.	Yes	No

I am not aware of any medical condition that would prohibit physical interaction such as handling or touching the dog. _____ (initial)

I, _____, give permission for _____ to participate in therapy dog visits at _____ School.

_____
Name of Parent or Guardian (Please print)

_____
Date

_____
Signature of Parent or Guardian

TEACHERS AND DOG THERAPY TEAMS

Dear Parents:

We, in Room 106 are hoping to participate this year in the Therapy Dogs International Program. This program assigns registered therapy dogs to enhance our educational environment. Beginning on [Date] or as soon as the district clears volunteer Barbara Vokatis to visit classrooms, we hope to welcome Barbara and her therapy dog Carmel into our classroom.

Barbara and Carmel will visit and participate with us weekly during our Language Arts time. Sometimes the students will be reading to Carmel, and other times Carmel will be part of their journal or creative writing time.

Student participation with the therapy dog team will be based on their comfort level.

I'm very excited to be able to participate in this program. Before the therapy dog team begins visits, we need permission from you for your child to participate. Please sign and return the permission slip below by [Date].

More information about the Therapy Dogs International program is available by contacting the therapy dog owner at ….

Sincerely,

_____

TEACHERS AND DOG THERAPY TEAMS

Place a checkmark on each preceding blank to indicate that you are granting permission.

I give permission for photographs of my child to potentially be used in:

    —— The school

    —— Newspaper and magazine articles

    —— Social media pages

    —— Photographs may be used, but not identify my child by name

Parent name: (please print) _____

Parent Signature: _____

REFERENCES

Allington, R. (2013). What really matters when working with struggling readers. *The Reading Teacher, 66*(7), 520-53.

American Kennel Club. (n.d.). *What is a therapy dog?* https://www.akc.org/sports/title-recognition-program/therapy-dog-program/what-is-a-therapy-dog/

Amsterlaw, J., Lagattuta, K. H., & Meltzoff, A. N. (2009). Young children's reasoning about the effects of emotional and physiological states on academic performance. *Child Development, 80*(1), 115-133. https://doi.org/10.1111/j.1467-8624.2008.01249.x

Baird, R., Grové, C., & Berger, E. (2022) The impact of therapy dogs on the social and emotional wellbeing of students: a systematic review. *Educational and Developmental Psychologist, 39*(2), 180-208, DOI: 10.1080/20590776.2022.2049444

Barker, S. B., & Dawson, K. S. (1998). The effects of animal-assisted therapy on anxiety ratings of hospitalized psychiatric patients. *Psychiatric Services, 49,* 797–801. doi:10.1176/ps.49.6.797

Bassette, L. A., & Taber-Doughty, T. (2013). The effects of a dog reading visitation program on academic engagement behavior in three elementary students with emotional and behavioral disabilities: A single case design. *Child & Youth Care Forum, 43,* 239–256. doi:10.1007/s10566-013-9197-y

Beck, L., & Madresh, E. (2008). Romantic partners and four-legged friends: An extension of attachment theory to relationships with pets. *Anthrozoös, 21,* 43–56. doi:10.2752/089279308X274056

Beetz, A., Julius, H., Turner, D., Kotrschal, K. (2012). Effects of social support by a dog on stress modulation in male children with insecure attachment. *Front Psychol, 3*, 352.

Beetz, A. M. (2015). *How animals in schools can support learning*. Retrieved from http://www.animalimpact.org/wp-content/uploads/2015/11/Keynote-Beetz.pdf.

Bergesen F. J. (1989). *The effects of pet facilitated therapy on the self-esteem and socialization of primary school children*. Presented at the 5th International Conference on the relationship between humans and animals. Monaco.

Booten, A. E. (2011). *Effects of animal-assisted therapy on behavior and reading in the classroom* (Undergraduate thesis). Retrieved from http://mds.marshall.edu/cgi/viewcontent.cgi?article=1023&context=etd

Braun, C., Stangler, T., Narveson, J., & Pettingell, S. (2009). Animal-assisted therapy as a pain relief intervention for children. *Complementary Therapies in Clinical Practice, 15*, 105–109. doi:10.1016/j.ctcp.2009.02.008

Briggs, R. (2003). Paws for reading: An innovative program uses dogs to help kids read better. *School Library Journal, 49*(6), 43. Retrieved from http://www.slj.com/2003/06/literacy/paws-for-reading-an-innovative-program-uses-dogs-to-help-kids-read-better/

Burns, R., & DiLonardo, M. J. (2014). READing paws: For giving young readers confidence (and cuddles). *Atlanta Magazine, 54*(5), 110. Retrieved from http://www.atlantamagazine.com/2014/reading-paws/

Coakley, A. B., & Mahoney, E. K. (2009). Creating a therapeutic and healing environment with a pet therapy program. *Complementary Therapies in Clinical Practice, 15*, 141–146. doi:10.1016/j.ctcp.2009.05.004

Darling-Hammond, L. (2000). Teacher quality and student achievement. *Education Policy Analysis Archives, 8*, 1-1.

Dunlap, V. M. (2010). *Canine assisted therapy and remediating reading: A review of literature*. (Master's thesis). Retrieved from http://www.nmu.edu/sites/DrupalEducation/files/UserFiles/Files/PreDrupal/SiteSections/Students/GradPapers/EdSpecialist/Dunlap_Vicki_EP.pdf

Friedmann, E., Katcher, A., Thomas, S., Lynch J, & Messene P. (1983). Social interaction and blood pressure: Influence of animal companions. *The Journal of Nervous and Mental Disease, 171*(8), 461–465. https://doi.org/10.1097/00005053-198308000-00002J

Garnto, M. (2014, March). *PAWS for reading: A free strategy that works*. Paper presented at the Virginia State Reading Association, Roanoke, Virginia. Retrieved from http://marilyngarnto.weebly.com/uploads/2/7/8/6/27862403/therapy_dogs.pdf

Gawlinski, A., & Steers, N. (2005). *Dogs ease anxiety, improve health status of hospitalized heart failure patients* (American Heart Association Abstract 2513). Retrieved from https://www.uclahealth.org/pac/Documents/volunteering/PACArticle.pdf

Goe, L., & Stickler, L. M. (2008). *Teacher quality and student achievement: Making the most of recent research*. TQ Research & Policy Brief. National comprehensive center for teacher quality.

Griess, J. O. (2010). *A canine audience: The effect of animal-assisted therapy on reading progress among students identified with learning disabilities* (Doctoral dissertation). Available from ProQuest Dissertations and Theses database. (UMI No. 3425685)

Guthrie, J. T. (2004). Teaching for literacy engagement. *Journal of Literacy Research, 36*, 1–28. doi:10.1207/s15548430jlr3601_2

Hall, S. S., Gee, N. R., & Mills, D. S. (2016). Children reading to dogs: A systematic review of the literature, *PLoS ONE, 11*(2), e0149759. https://doi.org/10.1371/journal.pone.0149759

Jalongo, M. R., Astorino, T., & Bomboy, N. (2004). Canine visitors: The influence of therapy dogs on young children's learning and well-being in classrooms and hospitals. *Early Childhood Education Journal, 32*, 9–16. doi:10.1023/B:ECEJ.0000039638.60714.5f

Le Roux, M. C., Swartz, L., & Swart, E. (2014). The effect of an animal-assisted reading program on the reading rate, accuracy and comprehension of Grade 3 students: A randomized control study. *Child & Youth Care Forum, 43*, 655–673. doi:10.1007/s10566-014-9262-1

Mackey, M. (2019). Visualization and the vivid reading experience. *Jeunesse: Young People, Texts, Cultures, 11*(1), 38-58.

Nevo, E. & Vaknin-Nusbaum, V. (2020) Enhancing motivation to read and reading abilities in first grade. *Educational Psychology, 40*(1), 22-41, DOI: 10.1080/01443410.2019.1635680

Sorin, R., Cook, J., & Brooks, T. (2015). The impact of the classroom canines program on children's reading, social and emotional skills, and motivation to attend school. *The International Journal of Literacies, 22*(2), 23-35.

Uvnäs-Moberg, K. (2011). *Oxytocin Factor: With a New Foreword: Tapping the Hormone of Calm, Love and Healing.* London, UK: Pinter and Martin Ltd.

Uvnäs-Moberg, K., Handlin, L., & Petersson, M. (2015). Self-soothing behaviors with particular reference to oxytocin release induced by non-noxious sensory stimulation. *Frontiers in Psychology, 5,* 1529. https://doi.org/10.3389/fpsyg.2014.01529

Viau, R., Arsenault-Lapierre, G., Fecteau, S., Champagne, N., Walker, C.D., Lupien, S. (2010). Effect of service dogs on salivary cortisol secretion in autistic children. *Psychoneuroendocrinology, 35*(8), 1187–1193.

Vokatis, B., & Zhang, J. (2016). Characterizing the identity of three innovative teachers engaging in sustained knowledge building. *Frontline Learning Research, 4*(1), 58-77. https://files.eric.ed.gov/fulltext/EJ1101458.pdf

Vokatis, B. (2021). *From unruly to therapy dog: The amazing journey.* Independently published.

Vokatis, B. (2021). *The amazing power of dog therapy: How my therapy dog transformed children's learning.* Independently published.

Wigfield, A., Gladstone, J. R., & Turci, L. (2016). Beyond cognition: Reading motivation and reading comprehension. *Child Development Perspectives, 10*(3), 190-195.

Wilson C. C. (1991). The pet as an anxiolytic intervention. *The Journal of nervous and mental disease, 179*(8), 482–489. https://doi.org/10.1097/00005053-199108000-00006

Zhang, J., Vokatis, B., Sun, Y. (2023). Literacy for knowledge building in two partnering science classrooms. In Paulo Blikstein et al. (Eds.), *Proceedings of the International Conference of the Learning Sciences*, Montreal, QC: The International Society of the Learning Sciences (ISLS).

INTERVIEW WITH THERAPY DOG TEAMS

Introduction to the interview:

In order to enrich the perspective on therapy dogs and their incredible work presented in this book, we interviewed three therapy dog teams and asked them some questions to elicit their perspectives.

Marcia is a former teacher who volunteers with her wonderful therapy dog. Marcia's therapy dog is a golden retriever named Charlie. Emily is a current teacher who brings her own therapy dog to her classroom. Her therapy dog, Oakley, is a goldendoodle. Erica is a school counselor whose therapy dog provides therapy for children in her counseling practice in school. Her dog is also named Charlie, and he is a mixed breed rescue dog.

I encourage you to read this interview to learn more about the incredible potential this kind of therapy has as well as great ideas about minimizing risks that prevent some schools from providing valuable dog therapy to many children.

Interview with Marcia, Emily, and Erica

Barbara: Good morning, everyone, and thank you for agreeing to do this interview! What would you say would be the major benefits of dog therapy in terms of comfort, calmness, de-stressing, and other typical sorts of therapeutic aspects?

Emily: I initially got Oakley for my co-taught inclusion classroom in Albany, New York. I had students with various different abilities and disabilities, along with general education children in this classroom. Oakley was really calming for some of my students that had a lot of physical and emotional needs.

A lot of those students would shove a desk, run out of the room, or hide if they got frustrated or upset. They showed their frustrations very physically. Having Oakley in the classroom opened the conversation up with students to say something like, "I see you're frustrated. I can see that you are trying to run out of the classroom and you are pushing your desk. And if you want to have Oakley in the classroom, we have to have a calm body. We have to have a quiet voice." So just his presence was calming.

Marcia Whiteside Hayden and Charlie, Instagram: @charliethetherapy

Marcia: I can agree with that. It's so interesting to watch the dog and the children interact with one another. Charlie perceives the emotions - when he goes in a classroom, he almost always seems to be gravitating toward one child. He interacts with all of the students, but he'll usually interact with one of the children more. And more times than not, I have teachers later coming back to me saying the child that Charlie went to was the one we were most concerned about.

Erica: In my role as the school counselor, most often kids would spend time with the dog in a one-on-one setting in my office. In those cases, students had trauma, and were immediately more relaxed and enjoyable when Charlie was present. Some of them are looking for a reason to leave class, but they're so much more open to talking and discussing what's going on when he is present.

Marcia: In one case, one of the students I worked with had actually abused animals before. Charlie went to him, gave him his paw, gave him a nudge on the side of the face, and I saw the child soften. I see things like that all the time - there have been just so many times where teachers come back and say that the child was having a hard time and struggling.

Another time we were actually waiting to go into a classroom and a child came out of the office and had been crying. When he saw Charlie, he kind of came to him and I said, "Would you like to pet him?" And he said "Yeah," knelt down, and started to share why he had been crying, while petting the dog. I don't remember the exact details, but I do remember that once he started touching the dog, he began to talk about an incident that happened at home. When I see that tactile-kinesthetic and emotional connection coming together, I know it's amazing what's happening between a therapy dog and a child.

Erica: I would also include my Charlie as a form of redirection. So, if we had a student in class who was having a meltdown, even a few instances where the room had to be cleared and the entire class was out because the student was a danger to their peers. I would always phrase it as "Charlie needs to go potty. Can you help me take him for a walk?" They would then view that as an opportunity to get out of the situation and then decompress, and then we can go back to discuss what it was that was causing them to be so upset in the classroom. So his presence alone was just very calming to the students and I feel like it made them a lot more open to discussing their feelings.

Marcia: I've been in special education classrooms and children get very excited when we come in, and when we get there and they touch the dog, they relax. Those are the types of things you see transpiring between the dog and children, and Charlie is very sensitive to that - that's why I think he's a therapy dog. I learned that not all dogs can be therapy dogs. I learned that with my other dog, Jackson, because Jackson had the same training Charlie's had but can't settle down. He's just a really happy boy. Charlie settles. You have to have the dog with the right temperament and that's critical.

Emily: I did have some students with special needs, particularly ones with social anxiety after the pandemic. Oakley's presence has been really nice because it gives the kids that little bit of excitement when they know he's coming in. They like to sit with him, talk to him and they help take care of him because they like to brush him. It gives them that excitement to be at school, it gives them something to look forward to, and his presence is just very calming for the kids, which is really cool.

For these students, it gave them that piece of reflection to be mindful of the dog and take efforts to make sure that they didn't scare the dog. That was a first step where the kids would say to themselves, "Oakley can come in if I have a safe body." From there, we started working on showing our using words. For example, petting Oakley and telling Oakley how they're feeling. So it kind of opened up that door where instead of just physically expressing themselves, they were then starting to be able to verbally express themselves.

Barbara: Do you have any examples of where a student was able to express themselves after Oakley started coming?

Emily: I have a little girl who is nervous to read and she would read out loud to Oakley instead of reading in front of the class. I would have her come up when the kids were at lunch, so just having him there has been very calming. And those kids that have a little bit of social anxiety or a little bit of nervousness in the classroom, they're able to then practice those situations with Oakley, whether it's reading or talking to him or whatever it might be.

Barbara: Thank you all for your responses and your stories. When you go on therapy visits, are these visits also connected to teaching and learning? What kind of effects have you seen in that regard?

Emily: The first time that I brought Oakley into a classroom, he would be with me all day long. On my breaks, when the kids are in music or lunch or anything like that, I'd take him into other classrooms. So the first time I go in, I typically introduce the students to Oakley. I explain to them what a therapy dog is. I show them some of Oakley's tricks because they always want to know what the tricks are. A lot of times they'll read to him - that's very popular.

Erica: I'm trying to put myself back in the role of a classroom teacher - I did teach for seven years and, if I were to go back and have him with me as a teacher, it would be such an engaging thing for the kids to have a dog in the building. You could do math - you could talk about paw prints, how many pieces of food or treats he's eating. Actually, my last year of teaching, my whole classroom was dog themed. I had paw prints everywhere, so even just the manipulatives that the students were using in math were paw prints and dog themed.

Marcia: Charlie's main purpose is to be a reading dog, and as you know, reading is the foundation and the building blocks to all other content areas. When children are struggling as readers, they're going to struggle academically. With younger children, the teacher typically reads the story first and then the children go in small groups and then sit with Charlie and read a bit more. Of course, while they're reading, they're petting Charlie.

Barbara: What about reading with older children, Marcia?

Marcia: When reading with older children - 4th, 5th, and 6th grade - it's a little bit different. The teacher introduces the book - typically a chapter book - and that's where I've seen the greatest educational benefit. You would think some of these big boys would think it would be silly to sit on a rug and read to the dog, but they are just so excited and they start petting and reading to the dog. Even the ones who struggle, they're not intimidated by me being there because Charlie is there. The focus is on reading to him and if they need assistance, sometimes their peers help them. Sometimes I'll lean over and help. But as a whole, I see them wanting to read and that to me is a critical building block to their future. I've seen even some of the ones who are a little more shy and anxious to jump right in there. So I have really seen an educational benefit to that.

Barbara: Exactly. But what we actually see when we are there - the educational benefit is not so easy to capture, right?

Marcia: No, it's not. Sometimes it's just a moment, and sometimes it might be several minutes, but you see those moments happen and it's amazing. When you see the child being successful with reading and when they get excited about it, that's the teacher in me and it's just so powerful.

Oakley and Emily Galarneau

Emily: In my room, if the kids have work, I let them work around the classroom because sitting in their seats can sometimes be really difficult, especially for elementary students. I usually let them work with Oakley because he sits up near me. I have them work with him on the floor and they'll sit and do their work on a clipboard or on their

Chromebook. They'll usually write, read, or do math. A lot of times, it's almost like they kind of know that they get stressed out about a certain subject, so they'll ask to work with him. So typically, it's a lot of just them working next to him, whether it's in partner work, individual work, anything like that. But because the students can move around, pet the dog, and be less stressed, I can observe that they're actually learning better.

Barbara: I remember in our school, we had the theme of "kindness." The kids were asked about how they think Carmel shows that she is kind. They came up with those ideas and then they brainstormed ideas on things they could learn from her in terms of kindness, and then they wrote about it. One thing teachers could do with their classes is have them write about the dog, like a little story or like a little blog about how the therapy dog shows respect, integrity, collaboration, etc. or something like that.

Erica: That's a great idea, Barbara. Reading is important, but writing is also important.

Barbara: I agree. OK, next question. If you could rewrite the curriculum, what other activities would you like to see your dog participate in? Perhaps in different subjects as well?

Marcia: That's a good question. As a teacher, I would have loved to have a therapy dog in my classroom all day. It would have allowed children to include him as an additional resource in the room, especially with science, social studies, and other creative activities. There are ways to get the dog involved. It would just depend on that teacher.

I really would love to see our school system include Charlie to help bring up their test scores and where he would work more specifically with just a few readers and measure where they were academically before and after working with the dog. I feel like there would be great gains with reading and perhaps even writing, since it is a natural outpouring of reading. We've actually done some of that. Charlie was invited to an after-school program and the children wrote stories about him and then read them to him. There's just all kinds of avenues that you can go with this and it would carry over into the other subject areas as well.

Erica: There are so many things I think you could do with the dog in the building. I love what you did with the kids in writing, Marcia and Barbara. Some kids hate writing and it is such a struggle.

Marcia: I really liked what Emily said with letting students work around the classroom and with Oakley, and letting the kids guide their thinking in their learning. I've never really done an activity like that, so that would definitely be something that would be fun if the kids were able to do an activity based on their interest in Charlie. I haven't really done much with that because following the school's curriculum is something that you have to do. So opening up some sort of creative writing would be really cool, especially because the kids have a really hard time with writing. That might be something that would get them interested and excited about writing rather than feeling like they have writer's block where they're not sure what to write about.

Barbara: Exactly. Last year, I was reading a book to kids, and it was about my therapy dog, Carmel. The kids had an idea to write their own autobiographies. They saw me as Carmel's mom, their friend, but also an author. I was coming in every week for half an hour and helping them with different things like how to start a chapter. Everything was done in connection with the teacher. If we work more closely with teachers, we can actually do some amazing things with the dogs.

Marcia: Right. That's what I'm hoping to get towards. Right now, it's just an hour visit and interacting and touching, and children are learning more than just the academics. Children are learning about how to behave and interact with a dog, which is happening as the traditional academic curriculum is being taught.

Erica: I taught fifth and sixth grade and the teaching point of view is really difficult. I think it would be a lot of fun to do lessons from a point of view of Charlie's perspective on something. In one of the sixth grade standards, kids have to understand how the perspective of the author can change. For example, how would Charlie feel if there were no more bathroom breaks allowed?

Barbara: Time for a sad question, but an important one. How would you handle a difficult situation if your therapy dog passed away between visits?

Marcia: That's something that I've thought about before, because we never know. From my experience with working with children, they're resilient. And if there's one thing about dealing with animals, it's a good thing for children to have them around as pets because there are life lessons that go beyond just taking care of them, petting them, and loving them. There's dealing with grief when one of them passes away. And so, there's multiple avenues that I think could be addressed. For example, children love to draw pictures and Charlie gets pictures and stories constantly from when we visit. I would say to let the teacher and the owner talk about ways to let children express their feelings, because the owner is going to be grieving as well.

Maybe getting another one in there as quickly as possible can be an option because there's going to be a tremendous void. Just getting another dog coming in and interacting with them might help resolve those emotions and feelings. But this might not always be a good option. I'm going to get another puppy in the next couple years just simply because I know that Charlie can't do this forever and I just believe so much in what I see taking place and the value of a therapy dog in a classroom and helping children learn. I wish everyone could go on a visit with me, because I can only capture little snapshots of the amazing things that take place.

Emily: Until you asked that question, I haven't really ever thought about it, but how I would probably handle it is to talk about how we love Oakley so much and he had a really big impact on us; reflecting on those positive things that we learned from him, like kindness, patience, and different ways that we can cope with feeling sadness. I think it kind of opens up the door to talking about those bigger feelings that might be a little bit challenging to talk about.

Everyone's going to have someone in their life that passes away and using that as a teachable moment to teach the children to focus on the memories we have could even be a writing piece of some sort, or drawing pictures of them with Oakley, making slideshows of pictures with them, and kind of talking about their feelings and opening up. Those more difficult to talk about things that don't always have a place in school kind of gives them that opportunity to get those feelings out.

That compassion that they feel toward Oakley - I'm sure they have those feelings about their own animals and they can connect to themselves. So, while that would be a really hard situation and a sad thing to have to talk about, I think it would also open up a lot of opportunities to have those more difficult conversations with the students.

Charlie and Erica Brown, Instagram: @girland2vandogs

Erica: Honestly, I've also never thought about it. As a classroom teacher, I think I would have to address it with my class as a whole. When something is consistent in a child's life, you do need to be straightforward with them and tell them what's happened. But in my role as a school counselor where Charlie comes once a week and may not visit with every student in the school, I don't think I would tell them unless they were asking me where he's been. I think that would be most appropriate in my situation as a school counselor. But as a classroom teacher, I do think I would want to address it with my class as a whole.

Barbara: Let's say that only one student is allergic to dogs in the classroom, but no one else in the class is. How would you handle that type of situation?

Erica: I love this question because it has been such a non-issue for me. Charlie's a lab mix so he is full of dander and full of all the allergens. We have a couple students in my school who are allergic and I call their parents at the beginning of each year. I do an opt-out form - everybody's allowed to participate with Charlie unless the parents return the form, and then I call each of those parents.

We had two students who had an allergy and neither one of them returned the opt out form, so I called both parents and they both said it's not a big deal. They just needed to wash their hands afterwards. We also had a plan in place for kids who may have a severe allergy where they really don't even need to be in the room. The Google search that I did when I was presenting this to my Superintendent said that ultimately kids come in contact with more dander just from their peers in terms of clothes, shoes, and backpacks being in the room.

My plan, if we were to have a severe allergy, would be to have a job for that particular student where they could help in the office, not as a punishment. Going to the library to read isn't really fun when you know your whole class is doing something else fun. Kids love to be helpers. They love to make copies for teachers. They love to do annoying things like shred paper that we don't have time for. So just having a plan for a student who did have an allergy to be a helper and make sure that they're still enjoying their time when they're not in the classroom.

Emily: That's a great idea about allowing the allergic children to work in the office, Erica. As for my dog, Oakley is a goldendoodle, so his hair and saliva don't tend to bother a lot of people that typically would have an allergy. But when I was asking to bring him into school, I had to get permission from the nurse. The nurse went through her files and identified students that might have an allergy or reaction to the dog and helped call parents for permission and luckily, it didn't turn out to be a problem. The nurse just wanted to make sure that the kids would regularly wash their hands after they pet him.

Marcia: When I come into a classroom, the teachers let me know which children can't be photographed, which children that are allergic, or anything else that I need to know. Even on the last visit that Charlie made at the school, we came in and the one teacher let me know that a child is allergic to dogs, so he would be sitting at a distance and just observing. It is similar to swimming. Some people swim in the shallow end with water wings, some in the shallow end without them, and some in the deep end. If you are in the shallow end, you can still observe the people in the deep end.

I've had several different cases and they just watch, and the children are fine and handle it great. I think that's another one of those life lessons that we learned with animals. Sometimes we're allergic to them, sometimes we're not, and it just makes a difference in whether they can touch.

Barbara: What if a child is scared of dogs? How would you handle that?

Marcia: Depending on how scared they are, they usually sit back and watch. Last year in first grade we had a little boy and you could tell he was very much afraid. When Charlie comes into a room, he usually goes around and meets every child before we go to the rug and do our thing, but in this case, we just walked by the scared child, and he did not do any touching.

Another boy, when we got into circle time, he sat in a chair and he kept inching forward until finally he was on the rug. And then a few minutes later, everyone had touched the dog and you could see he wanted to as well. So, the teacher said, "Here, let me help you." And she took his hand, and bless his heart, his little hand was trembling and just touched the back of Charlie. Charlie didn't even really respond because he's touched so much, and the little boy kind of smiled and then he cried, you know?

The next time we came, I talked to the teacher and I arranged it so that Charlie made a special visit just to go see this little boy. We did this three different times to the point where the next time we're in the hallway, the little boy came up running to him. That was probably the most severe case of a child being afraid of the dog. The rest of them generally kind of stand back and they see everybody else and they see that the dog is not going to hurt them and they eventually move in. This little boy really struggled, but it was a true success story.

Barbara: So, it wasn't as scary, because I think that many schools might not even consider having therapy dogs in the classroom because they might be afraid that parents would not agree, but once you look at it in more depth and talk to the parents, it turns out that they can be in classrooms and there are quite a number of benefits.

Emily: Right, so you just find ways to make it work, and as far as children being scared, I actually had two students in my class this year who were scared of dogs, and I have pictures of them with Oakley now and they kind of overcame that fear, which was really cool.

Barbara: I had a situation like that too. There is a way of doing it. We don't just approach them with the dog right away. Once they see that the dog is nice, they start to warm up a little bit.

Emily: On the first day of school, a little boy in my class was like, "I'm really scared of dogs, but I know Oakley comes into school. I probably won't touch him." And I told him that's fine, and that I would keep him away from your desk and you look at him from afar. He was like, "OK, but it's my goal by the end of the year to pet him." And I said, "OK, that's a great goal." By the end of the first day, he had already walked over and gave him a little pat on the head. It's nice that the students have the opportunity to work on that kind of fear; if the dog had not come into school, they might go their whole life being scared. It's a cool opportunity for them.

Erica: I agree! At my school, there were a couple of parents who said their kids were afraid of Charlie. I actually had one mother who didn't return the opt out form, but she called me and told me that her son has autism and is afraid of being around dogs, but she wanted him to learn how to be around dogs. I had two other parents who shared that they didn't care if their boys were around the dog, but that they didn't want to be pushed to do it. I explained that it's always an option to pet the dog, and I would never force them to work with Charlie or be around him if they don't want to participate. They don't want to pet him, totally fine. I never push it.

My favorite story is about a student with autism who was afraid of dogs. He's at middle school now. This kiddo had two years with Charlie and he was Charlie's biggest fan. By the time he left, he was obsessed with him and just loved him. So, in a way, for those students who are afraid of dogs, it's also a teachable moment because you can show them how to interact with a dog safely. You know, how to engage with a dog and make it a more pleasant experience.

Emily: I've also had situations at my previous school where children from certain ethnicities or religions were not allowed to touch dogs. In those cases, I just didn't visit those classrooms or I would wait until that student was not in the classroom to come in. In other situations, groups of children would come visit my classroom during my lunch period so that the other kids didn't miss out so that they could see the therapy dog while still respecting the wishes of the other student.

Barbara: We talked about how a therapy's dog's presence has contributed to students becoming less afraid of them, but how does the presence of the dog help connect learning activities to the curriculum?

Marcia: Different states have different requirements. We have state standards and the teacher is aware of the standards that are being covered. In each visit you know what is being taught and the corresponding standards. The therapy dog is included in their lesson plans when he comes. And of course, having taught for so many years, I pretty much know what they are as well.

Sometimes they write little stories. And once it was writing a story about Charlie as a superhero and their adventures with Charlie. So, they were obviously using creativity, but they were using those writing skills that they had been taught in order to meet those narrative writing standards. Another time it was what was their favorite thing to do with Charlie, or if they could take Charlie anywhere, where would they go? There's just so many different ways. Some teachers actually have students write after Charlie's been there and describe their interaction and what they did with Charlie.

Barbara: That's awesome. And that is what improves those writing skills. So that is obviously part of the writing curriculum. What about things that aren't content-related, like social skills and emotional skills?

Emily: Definitely, the social-emotional piece is huge. We have a district curriculum for the social-emotional piece called Second Step. I'm someone that focuses a ton of my time and energy on building a positive, collaborative classroom. So, for me, I spent so much time at the beginning of the year working on questions like "What does it look like to be a good friend?", "What does it look like to be a good student?", and "How can we be empathetic with each other and ensure that students really feel comfortable and safe in the classroom?" Oakley definitely connects in that regard - kindness, talking about empathy, and calming strategies - you know, taking deep breaths, counting to 10, or talking to Oakley about being frustrated. He definitely plays a huge piece in our social-emotional curriculum with the district.

I definitely feel as though students coming back from the COVID-19 pandemic have had a higher level of anxiety, so having him there and teaching them those coping skills and teaching them those calming techniques has been really helpful. Kids know that if they're feeling stressed out, they can come in and pet Oakley. We have kids from different classrooms throughout the day. If they're having a hard time, they can spend five minutes with Oakley to help them calm down. He's a huge part of our social-emotional curriculum.

Erica: Adding on to what Emily said, I think it is what you make it. As a teacher, part of your job is to make the content interesting to the students. You can take any standard that you need to cover and incorporate a therapy dog. It's just a matter of being proactive and thinking ahead about how you can include him or her to make it relatable and engaging to the student.

Barbara: What about different classrooms? Are lessons differentiated based on different kinds of classrooms, especially educational resource rooms versus mainstream classrooms?

Marcia: Absolutely. The day I knew that Charlie was definitely going to be a therapy dog, I had taken "paw-ternity" leave. I still had about two more months of school, and so I took four weeks with my puppy, but I was back in the school very quickly with that puppy. I had one particular class that had an autistic child in it. And before Charlie met any other children, we went and got the autistic child and went into a small quiet room. He was so excited that Charlie was a boy, and I have one of the most amazing videos watching him interact with the child so gently. The interaction brought tears to my eyes. This is a true gift from God to have this animal. It's unbelievable.

Since Charlie has gotten older and more advanced with his training, we've been in multiple inclusion classrooms which are differentiated depending on the severity of their disability. He responds differently to each child and their needs.

As far as going into a special education classroom, the curriculum is differentiated and teachers still meet the standards, but it's meeting them on each student's level. When Charlie goes into a special education classroom, it's planned well in advance. The teachers know we're coming. Charlie knows that when he gets there, it's different. Usually, there are more paraprofessionals present. The interactions are mostly one-on-one, pretty much each child with Charlie. The stories are read to them like in the other classrooms and then they touch and they feel - again, that kinesthetic-tactile piece. It takes planning, it really does. You can certainly bring a dog into a classroom and walk them through, and that's wonderful, but to really have a successful program, it requires planning between the teachers, the administration and then the therapist or therapy team.

Barbara: Right, and like you said the differentiation also happens in the way the dog reacts to different children and their different needs.

Marcia: Absolutely. Because teachers had to learn how to differentiate, you know? But the dog doesn't. He does it naturally.

Erica: I agree that the therapy dogs naturally differentiate among students. My favorite spot in the building to let Charlie go in is our moderate to severe disability room. These are our students with the most severe disabilities, most of whom are non-verbal. That's my favorite room to go in, because the students just light up when Charlie comes in. There's one student who has high-needs autism and he's very sensory-based.

There's another student who got to the point where he didn't really want to play with Charlie, but he would just come up to him and take both his hands and scratch his fingers down Charlie's back, kind of like a spider. I just thought it was the cutest thing and that's all he wanted to do. He would leave after that. But even activities that the special education teacher did with her students, with the most severe needs - those kids were still so excited to show Charlie their artwork. They would be doing cutting activities and they would just hug him and hold it up and show it. So, it is differentiation, absolutely. Not a problem.

Barbara: Some of the lessons I mentioned where the kids wrote autobiographies were with second graders. Can something like that be done in middle and high school classrooms? Would they think it would be silly to be reading with a dog at those age levels?

Marcia: Middle school is where I spent the majority of my teaching career. I would have loved to have a therapy dog in my room all day!

And about a year and a half ago, we went to two different classrooms in middle school. It was more of a friendly visit and he interacted with the kids and they wanted to sit down and talk with him. I feel confident that there is plenty that could be done in middle school and in high school with therapy dogs, and not just showing up in a grief situation. I'm not making light of that by any means, but I think on an educational level as well as helping children learn and be successful, it would make a huge difference.

Emily: I know Marcia had mentioned middle school and you mentioned high school, Barbara. I think middle school and high school are some of the hardest years. Even having him as just a calming presence or having a dog as part of a research project, comparing therapy dogs versus service dogs. Things like that, it opens up a whole different world of interest for students, for sure.

Barbara: And again, it goes down to this interaction between the therapy dog team and the teacher working together to maybe try to figure out an activity together, right?

Emily: Oh, absolutely. We have two "strive" classrooms in our school that have students with a range of different abilities and disabilities. "Strive" is a special education classroom for students with greater needs. It stands for Structured Teaching Reinforced in a Visual Environment. It is for students with any disability who need a highly structured environment and visual support, in addition to instruction in social skills and self-regulation. Such students are served in a general education setting as much as possible. Some of the students are non-verbal. I'm not 100% sure of what their disabilities are.

A lot of them get so excited to see Oakley and you can see their little faces light up and they're working on those social skills, learning how to say words like hi and using their devices to be able to talk and express themselves. So, giving them something that's interesting to them and making them want to use those social skills is really cool. Every now and then they'll be working on taking a walk through the hallway, and Oakley just goes and sits out in the hallway and they give him a pet. They work on saying hi. They work on saying thank you or even just making eye contact for a second with Oakley. Huge things for them that seem very simple everyday things for us.

It's really cool that they're able to focus on some of those skills with Oakley, where it might be a little less intimidating rather than saying hi to an adult, which might be a little scary for them. Oakley's visits can impact a range of different people and a range of different students. He's there, whether it's for a quick five-second walk by or a kid who's afraid to read out loud to the class they can read to him. So definitely, different things can be done in different kinds of classrooms.

Barbara: I'm thinking about this writing activity where we ask kids to describe how Carmel is kind and how they would apply it to their own situation. This would be beneficial for every child, regardless of whether they have a disability or not.

Emily: True, that would be great for all kids, regardless of ability or disability. Barbara, do the kids ever have questions about Carmel when you are talking to them?

Barbara: Oh yes, plenty of great questions about her!

Emily: Yeah, the kids have such great questions about Oakley too, like why he is a therapy dog, and you can get into all of those reasons why or the different places he could go. It definitely opens the door to awesome conversations with students.

Barbara: That's interesting, because in terms of influencing curriculum, it really opens up the classroom to have more inquiry and possibly researching activities.

Erica: From a reading perspective, you can do it from a point of view. Carmel came from a breeder, right? Charlie came from a shelter. How can their perspectives overlap? There are so many different things in looking at different dogs. Many students have a pet, and everyone knows someone who has a pet. What would their different perspectives be?

Barbara: Exactly. I think that's awesome, and in middle and high school, students need to argue and persuade more. Students have to write, so how about looking at which dog could be better as a therapy dog, one from a breeder or one from a shelter?

Erica: There are so many people who are successful with this, so I don't think you can go wrong. I didn't have intentions of doing this with Charlie until my boss mentioned it, and I immediately knew that I had the perfect dog. I knew his temperament.

To me, I think it's a benefit if you go through the rescue and adopt an adult dog. You can window shop and look at all of these rescues and identify the character traits that you're looking for. And if you're patient, you can find the perfect dog for therapy work through rescue.

Fortunately, I already had the perfect one. He's wonderful, but a lot of people want to get the poodle mixes that are more hypoallergenic and I think that's great too. But there are ways to work around it if someone doesn't have the money or if you already have dogs.

Barbara: Do you think that certain ages or breeds of therapy dogs are better in classrooms?

Marcia: That's a good question because my experience is with golden retrievers. I would say it's all about temperament. I don't think the breed would matter. What matters is if they have the right temperament or personality, the ability to calm down and then interact and allow people to touch you and not get overly excited. That's not to say that they don't get excited in the classroom - Charlie can get excited, but he can also settle back down. I don't think the size of the dog matters either, it's really just about the temperament.

Barbara: I agree. However, there are a lot of golden retrievers that are therapy dogs actually.

Marcia: Because so many of them have that easy-going, laid-back temperament.

Emily: I noticed when I did Oakley's therapy dog class, there were all different kinds of breeds. There were really small dogs and there was a German shepherd who was about eight years old. There were definitely a bunch of golden retrievers - that seemed to be the most popular breed there. There were a couple golden doodles. I think any dog, as long as they're calm and good listeners and not jumpy, works in classrooms. It all depends on the training, not necessarily the breed.

For me, I liked that Oakley didn't shed just because I know that I wouldn't want dog hair all over me and I want to get all up in there and snuggle them and pet them. I liked the golden doodle because he's not going to cover the children with dog hair and he doesn't drool excessively either whereas a mastiff is going to drool and get hair everywhere. I think it just depends on your preference. I don't think any specific breed is better than another. I saw all different kinds of dogs and each dog has a different personality which can bring different conversations and experiences to the kids. I think it all depends on the training and how much time and effort you put into the dog.

Barbara: As far as the age of the dog, I would imagine that as long as the dog still finds joy in the therapy work, it would be okay, right?

Marcia: And as far as age, I don't think that matters either. I had Charlie interacting at eight and nine weeks and it was obvious to me already that he was the right dog. I learned very quickly at a young age, therapy dogs can't go that long. Charlie didn't get certified until 18 months because COVID hit, and at that point anything more than one hour in a visit was a lot. In a two-hour visit, we visited two classes and the first one was great, but the second class he was just kind of laying there.

Now, he can do two to three classes. The third class kind of pushes him a little bit. It just depends on the day. We try to keep it down to two classes and not more, and about two hours at the most. We also limit the number of visits in a week, because the dogs can burn out. I started noticing that Charlie was not interacting with people the way he had been. We had been doing five visits a week, so we took a week off. Now, we generally do two to three visits a week and he usually comes home and takes a nap afterwards.

Emily: I agree with you about knowing the dog's personality and how long they can be in a classroom for. Oakley is very calm, he's very chill. You know, another dog from Oakley's litter is a much different dog, still a golden doodle, but a much different personality. Still very friendly, just a little more excitable. You might have a dog that you put tons of time and energy into, but he still shouldn't be a therapy dog because he's too excited.

Barbara: The therapy owner has to look for the signs of tiredness, like when the dog is not enjoying it anymore and due to age. But generally, even older dogs, they can be therapy dogs too. There is no limitation of age.

Emily: I don't think so, no.

Barbara: I've heard stories about rescue dogs being taken from really bad situations that became incredible therapy dogs later. It's more about the demeanor of the dog rather than the breed or if the dog comes from rescue or not. I remember that in our therapy dog class, our teacher demonstrated many therapy tasks with her therapy dog. Before she demonstrated the tasks, she introduced her dog, told us he has been a therapy dog for 10 years, and told us about the rescue mission. We were all amazed to hear about this amazing outcome for this dog.

Erica: That sounds like a great overall experience for the dog.

Barbara: The last question is what happens if the dog were to bite a child?

Erica: Well, my short answer is that would never happen, but I know with the Alliance of Therapy Dogs, there are protocols that you have to follow if something like that were to happen. You have to notify the supervisor. If something like that were to happen, I really feel like it would be a result of me as the handler not following my guidelines and paying attention to his body language and making sure that he's not in a situation that's making him uncomfortable. So, I would follow those guidelines that are set forth by whatever organization you're working with. But as long as I'm doing my part as the handler, that wouldn't happen.

Marcia: A dog biting a child is one of my greatest fears. You have to remember that they are animals. A large part of it is educating children but always being aware of things yourself. When I first started visiting classrooms, teachers would pull out a chair for me to sit on, but I wanted to sit right next to the dog to catch something just in case something were to happen.

I did once have a rather large group, in a general education class. There might have been about seven students there. I try to keep the groups to five. One child did something to Charlie; I didn't see it happen but I happened to turn my head and saw Charlie turned and jumped but there was no biting. Because of that, I have restricted the number of children in a group that we can take because I'm constantly observing him and them and what's going on and what's going on around us. So, I think it's incumbent upon us as the handler to really make sure that you are aware of what's going on to prevent it. I think prevention is the greatest key to that.

Emily: That's where that insurance thing is so important. You have to keep your dog up to date on vaccines, their vet visits, keeping your therapy dog insurance and paperwork up to date is so important. The school will have your back, but you have to follow the rules too.

Marcia: That's very true! With our therapy association, if something happens, we are required to end the session immediately, remove the dog, and contact them. So, I would say no matter what you're doing, if something like that happens, everything stops and you address the child and you address the dog and remove the dog from there. And then I guess it would be an evaluation process at that point. My prayer is that this never transpires and that's why I take the precautions I take so it doesn't happen. But you have to always know that they are animals and it could.

Barbara: Schools have rules too as far as reporting incidents. In elementary schools, kids can sometimes do unexpected things to dogs.

Emily: Right. They're still animals. It might be the most well-behaved dog you've ever met, but they're still animals and they're unpredictable. So, you have to follow the rules. The kids ask me all the time, "Can I feed Oakley a snack?" And I'm like, no, you cannot feed Oakley. That's part of the rules - I have to sign a contract that says I will not let anyone else feed him. It's part of the training, he's taught to only take food from the handler, and he's taught not to take things up off the floor. It's so important to make sure that you're following those rules, because if I said to a child like, "Oh yeah, sure. Give them a treat" and then he was to bite the child's hands - well, I went against the therapy dog rules, and then I might get in trouble for that.

Barbara: Thank you very much for the interview, Marcia, Emily, and Erica. It's clear we all use include therapy dogs in the classroom to great success!

Conclusion for the interview:

We feel that there are three main takeaways from this interview. The first one is the very apparent benefit of including dog therapy in schools. All the interviewed therapy dog teams highlighted this aspect in their responses. They all discussed amazing levels of comfort, de-stressing, and higher academic performance, which is all related to the calming presence of therapy dogs and how the students interact with them.

All the interviewed teams also provided concrete solutions to potential problems that might arise, such as allergies, possible dog biting, and more. It is evident that such dogs need to be registered in appropriate therapy organizations and the therapy dog owner needs to have a thorough understanding of issues and responses to potential problems, as required by the therapy organization and the school. These interviewers also spoke about issues like opting out forms and speaking individually with parents to address individual concerts.

Another theme in these conversations touches on future research and innovation with dog therapy. All therapy dog teams expressed an interest in involving their dogs in newer types of activities, in which dog therapy is more closely connected with learning, such as writing or math. More research in this area would be very beneficial in order to learn more about the benefits of dog therapy.

www.ingramcontent.com/pod-product-compliance
Lightning Source LLC
Chambersburg PA
CBHW052148070526
44585CB00017B/2029